THE
LAKE
MOUNTAINS
ONE

Skiddaw and Blencathra
to Black Combe

Also by Terry Marsh

The Summits of Snowdonia
The Mountains of Wales
The Lake Mountains: Two

British Library Cataloguing in Publication Data

Marsh, Terry
 The Lake Mountains: a walker's guide to
 the 600-metre summits and other fells of
 the Lake District.
 1. Mountains – England – Lake District –
 Guide-books   2. Lake District (England) –
 Description and travel – Guide-books
 I. Title
 914.27′804858   DA670.L1

ISBN 0-340-38786-6

All photographs by the author

Typeset in Great Britain for Hodder and Stoughton Limited, Mill Road, Dunton Green, Sevenoaks, Kent by Rowland Phototypesetting Limited, Bury St Edmunds, Suffolk and printed by St Edmundsbury Press Limited, Bury St Edmunds, Suffolk. Hodder and Stoughton Editorial Office: 47 Bedford Square, London WC1B 3DP.

THE
LAKE
MOUNTAINS

ONE

Skiddaw and Blencathra
to Black Combe

TERRY MARSH

Hodder & Stoughton

LONDON SYDNEY AUCKLAND TORONTO

Acknowledgements

I have been greatly assisted by Allan Rimmer who read the draft manuscript for me, and proffered much helpful advice from his considerable knowledge of the Lake District. Tim Owen, in the Ordnance Survey at Southampton, gave invaluable assistance in checking all the heights and map references of my initial research, and constantly encouraged me to keep going. The library and archival staff of the Department of Leisure in Wigan produced all the books and information I asked for. And in the same way the staff of the Ordnance Survey Record Map Library made mounds of maps available to me, for which I am immensely grateful.

I am obliged to Walt Unsworth for permission to quote from *The High Fells of Lakeland*, and to the many authors detailed in the Bibliography, for the hours of pleasurable reading, I am loath to call it research, they have given me.

A special thanks goes to all those who accompanied me on the fells, for I was seldom alone, especially to Albert who first took to the mountains at the tender age of sixty-five!

Finally, my thanks to my wife, Frances, who tolerated my neglect of household responsibilities at weekends with good grace, and during weekday evenings as I disappeared to my study, when only the constant demand for coffee and outbursts of self-inflicted invective told her there was still a man about the house.

TM

Contents

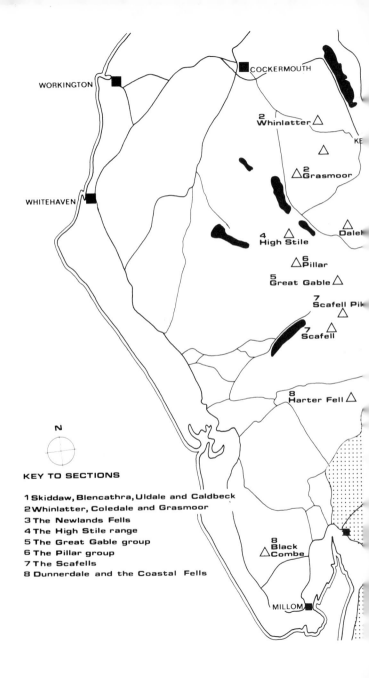

WORKINGTON

COCKERMOUTH

2
Whinlatter △

△ KE

2
△ Grasmoor

WHITEHAVEN

△
Dale

4 △
High Stile

△
6
Pillar

5 △
Great Gable

7
Scafell Pik
△

7 △
Scafell

8
Harter Fell △

N

KEY TO SECTIONS

1 Skiddaw, Blencathra, Uldale and Caldbeck
2 Whinlatter, Coledale and Grasmoor
3 The Newlands Fells
4 The High Stile range
5 The Great Gable group
6 The Pillar group
7 The Scafells
8 Dunnerdale and the Coastal Fells

8
△ Black
Combe

MILLOM

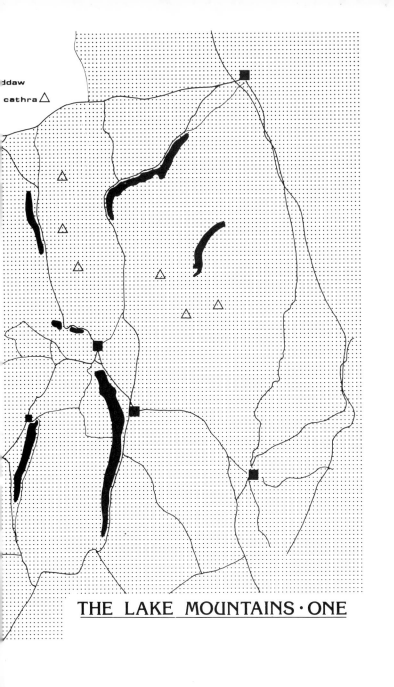

ddaw

cathra △

THE LAKE MOUNTAINS · ONE

Causey Pike and the pastureland of the Newlands valley.

Introduction

It was in the Lake District that I first set foot on a mountain, and from here that I learned to love not only the Lakeland fells, but the high mountain uplands throughout Britain and Europe. On that first, autumnal, encounter I walked from Keswick to Stair and ascended Causey Pike over Rowling End. Many of the higher mountains were shrouded in mist, and my attention focused northward on the Vale of Keswick, a scene of remarkable beauty to my eager, receptive mind, no less inspiring when last revisited during the preparation of this book, and probably not much different from the scene which in 1766 caused Dr. John Brown, the popular divine, to address a letter to Lord Lyttelton in which he dilated with some eloquence upon the beauties of the Vale of Keswick, or that which greeted the poet Gray, who in the autumn of 1769 "passed six days lap'd in Elysium" as he toured around the northern end of the district, Derwentwater and Borrowdale.

The next day I walked to Watendlath, and ascended the short distance to overlook Rosthwaite and a landscape of such russet vibrancy that the vision of it will still spring clear long after the photograph I took at the time has faded.

I returned home intoxicated by images of wild and rugged splendour, of range after range of mountains, of cascading cataracts and deep, dark-eyed tarns, of wooded dales and windswept moors, of nature's raw and unremitting challenge. And I wonder now, in retrospect, how the early travellers felt, whether they experienced the forces I encountered, and whether I could ever have had the adventurousness they displayed when first they set foot on the Lake Mountains: at least I went knowing that someone had been before me.

Such records as exist of mountain walking in the Lake District date from the latter part of the eighteenth century when a number of visitors tackled the ascent of Skiddaw. It was an era when the romantic was seen in terms of nature's grandeur, and 'horrid' was an acceptable term to apply to a crag. Horror and mountains were inextricably linked, and the fortitude of those pioneers must have been great. They were very much a minority and regarded as cranks. But writers quickly came to see mountains as objects to be ascended for enjoyment and for the magnificent panoramas they afforded. Hutchinson, the Cumberland historian, climbed Skiddaw in the early 1770s, and commented: "The prospect which we gained from the eminence very well rewarded the fatigue." The same mountain and its neighbours were often ascended on fell ponies, and ponies were still available for hire from Grasmere as late as 1914.

More visitors, who, according to Wordsworth, "flocked to the Lake country in all the spirit of adventurers, not a little oppressed by their own hardihood, and furnished forth with all the necessary emotional equipment", led to more accounts of the terrors and splendours of the place, culminating in 1823 with the first true guide-book, produced and published by Jonathan Otley, a Keswick guide, and regarded by many as the father of Lakeland geology. It carried the customary lengthy title: A Concise Description of the English Lakes, The Mountains in their vicinity, And the Roads by which they may be visited; With Essays on Mineralogy and Geology, on Meteorology, the Floating Island on Derwent Lake, and the Black-Lead Mine in Borrowdale, and Map of the District. Unlike other books, which were purely descriptive of the scenery, Otley's was the first "directing the tourist through the most eligible paths".

The Lake District is unique; here there is a remarkable assemblage of mountains, or 'fells' as they are known, so compact they could, according to that Highland *stravaiger* Hamish Brown, fit nicely in to Rannoch Moor in Scotland, and yet showing such remarkable diversity that they offer something for everyone. It is a region of old, hard rocks, repeatedly uplifted as the earth's crust moved, and then worn down again by erosion and weathering. They comprise, as Jonathan Otley described in the *Lonsdale Magazine* as long ago as 1820, a threefold division of rocks, two great slaty sedimentary groups separated by volcanic rocks. The oldest of the slates are the Skiddaw Slates, dating from Ordovician times, that is, up to 530 million years ago, but there are also many Silurian Slates – Stockdale Shales, Coniston Flags and Grits, Bannisdale Slates and Kirkby Moor Flags – dating from 440 million years ago. The volcanic rocks which separate the two slate groups, the Borrowdale Volcanic Series, were ejected from volcanic vents during the Ordovician period, and the later Silurian Slates laid down on top of them. The whole was then submerged in an ancient Carboniferous sea (about 300 million years ago), and later uplifted into the desert environment of the Triassic period (up to 225 million years ago).

As a result of this amazing geological mish-mash, the geologist will find a tremendous variety of stratified and unstratified rocks, from granite to carboniferous beds. But it isn't only the geologist who will be in his element. The botanist will be spellbound by the wealth of plant-life, the ornithologist by a richness of bird-life that can produce over ninety species in a single week. The anti-quary, too, will not be disappointed, Lakeland having been inhabited from the earliest times: druid circles and Pictish forts tell of a prehistoric presence; Roman camps and roads abound; runic crosses evidence the Nordic influence, which has left its mark in so many place-names; while local poets and prose-writers have recorded the life and character of the area.

Until the middle of the nineteenth century, much of England seems to have taken a persistently Philistine view of Lakeland. Mountains meant bad roads, poor accommodation, if any, the fear of being robbed, and the prospect, very real, of losing one's way. But it is a popular mistake that it was Wordsworth and Southey who *made* the Lake District for tourists. "An old admirer, one of the first who taught our prosaic forefathers to look for less tame models of the picturesque, was the poet Gray." Hutchinson's *Excursion to the Lakes*, first published in 1773, preceded Wordsworth's *Guide to the Lakes* by thirty-seven years; while Gray's own *Journal in the Lakes*, written in 1769, was published in 1775.

But it is to the modern fell-walker that this book is addressed; to those who seek out solitude and tranquil beauty, and those who share my deep love of a remarkable region, whose ambience attracts tens, hundreds of thou-sands each year.

There will be those who criticise this mass invasion of the hills, complaining that it has destroyed one of their intrinsic charms – solitude; but, in the words of the

National Park Guide, "the discriminating walker will know where and when to escape the crowds and will not begrudge others the opportunity for a fuller enjoyment of the National Park." This book concentrates very largely on the popular routes, though I have delved into some of the quieter recesses to offer alternative walks for those who wish to explore. Even so, there are so many different ways of tackling virtually every fell in Lakeland, that to cover them all takes at least eight volumes, as Alfred Wainwright has admirably demonstrated, and even then the skilled walker can work out more ways to every summit, without being "harassed at every turn by howling herds of unappreciative trippers" – as Haskett Smith complained, in 1894!

But it isn't only the summits which are the appeal of the Lake Mountains, it is their wealth of ridges, a factor contributing greatly to the unity and beauty of the area, as Wordsworth observed:

> and, first, of the MOUNTAINS. Their forms are endlessly diversified, sweeping easily or boldly in simple majesty, abrupt and precipitous, or soft and elegant. In magnitude and grandeur they are individually inferior to the most celebrated of those in some other parts of this island; but, in the combinations which they make, towering above each other, or lifting themselves in ridges like the waves of a tumultuous sea, and in the beauty and variety of their surfaces and colours, they are surpassed by none.

In this book I have grouped these mountains, quite arbitrarily, into eight sections. (The companion volume comprises seven further sections.) This grouping is for the reader's convenience, and does not reflect any wish to impose a superficial regularity on a region that would frustrate my task before it even began. Any such delineation in any event is open to criticism, as is the way I have determined which summits should be included in the main Table of 600-metre summits, and which in the Appendix. It's all entirely subjective.

The Ordnance Survey obliges us now to think in terms of metric heights and distances. Gone are the 2000-feet summits with which many generations, including my own, are familiar, virtually all the maps are now metric. So if you want your mountains in feet, tough! And does it matter anyway? Height alone is no real criterion; as someone once said, we have elevated mere altitude to an unmerited eminence. To some extent I've tried to avoid that; 600 metres is tolerably close to the meaningless 2000 feet someone thought up a long time ago, but I haven't excluded any summits just because they didn't measure up. Why cut off your nose to spite your face?

Without doubt, in the last two hundred years society has come a long way in its appreciation of our mountain heritage, but it is easy to forget that the mountains have changed little, if at all, in that time, and will be much the same long after I am (hopefully) roaming the hills of Paradise. The terror felt by our ancestors, the dangers and difficulties are still there. It is our attitudes which have changed, and sometimes I fear we are becoming too glib in our approach to, and respect for, the hills. From time to time I have been lulled into rhapsodising about the fells, but we must never forget that they can bring tragedy as well as joy. As the late Don Whillans put it: "The mountains give, and the mountains take."

Explanatory Notes

None of the routes described presents technical problems in good weather conditions in summer. In the main they are walks, not climbs, though a few – the Napes Traverse of Great Gable and Sharp Edge, for example – call for the ability to scramble, while one – Broad Stand – actually does require rock climbing skill. Where there are problems of this nature, I have said so in the text. The majority of the walks can also be completed in good winter conditions, though crampons may be required from time to time. But in winter, with snow and ice on the ground, an ice-axe is always essential, as is the knowledge to use it properly.

I have assumed throughout the book that readers are competent navigators, skilled in map and compass technique, and know how to clothe and protect themselves effectively against the weather. It is foolhardy to even think of venturing into mountainous terrain without these fundamental skills.

Table 1 – set out on pages 17–21 – lists, in order of altitude, all elevations of 600 metres or more in the whole of the Lake District, not merely those covered in this volume, with a minimum of 30 metres of re-ascent from all directions, including summits of sufficient topographical merit with less re-ascent. It also contains an appendix of all other summits over 600 metres with less than 30 metres of re-ascent, though I have not included elevations which have no measurable re-ascent, e.g. High Pike on the Fairfield Horseshoe. The lists are based on a survey of the latest 1:10000 scale Ordnance Survey maps.

Maps In the preparation of Table 1 I have used 1:10000 maps in order to pinpoint exactly where the highest point on any summit lies – it isn't always the trig point! – and so that I can carefully measure the amount of re-ascent. Map references are to the nearest 100 metres when converted for use on 1:50000 maps.

The Lake District has the distinction of being almost entirely covered by four excellent Outdoor Leisure Maps to a scale of 1:25000 (or 2½ inches to a mile), and although all my references relate to the conventional 1:50000 maps, which are also more convenient for carrying on the hills, the reader will benefit from looking at these much more detailed maps on which many of the features I have mentioned as being "not named on the 1:50000 map" are clearly identified.

Other maps do exist which I must mention in passing. These are produced by Harvey Map Services, originally for use in the Karrimor International Mountain Marathon. They are to a scale of 1:40000 (1½ inches to a mile), and are printed on a waterproof material known as Duxbak. Because they were prepared for a specific purpose they do not cover the entire area of the Lake District, and only relate to the Helvellyn area, Borrowdale, the Scafells, and Coniston/Windermere.

Heights Heights are the latest available from the Ordnance Survey and may occasionally differ from those on published maps. There are also a few instances where a summit has two points of the same height, some distance apart. Where this occurs I have supplied two map references.

If there is no height available, the height shown in the Tables is that of the highest contour ring. In these cases the height is followed by the letter c.

Distances and Ascent These are approximate and have been rounded up or down, but they are sufficiently accurate to allow you to calculate times using Naismith's or other rules.

Paths There are numerous paths throughout the Lake District, far more than I have detailed in this book. It should be noted however that *any reference to paths or other lines of ascent does not imply that a right of way exists.*

Names The Ordnance Survey spelling has been used throughout, taken from the 1:10000 maps, and I have included alternative names generally in use (in parentheses). If there is no name on any map, then the name commonly accepted either locally or among hill-walkers has been used. In the absence of anything, a rare occurrence in Lakeland, the expression 'Unnamed summit' has been adopted, next to which, for identification purposes, has been given the name of the nearest named summit.

Sections and Section names are quite arbitrary, and centre on one or more principal fells or other geographical features. No one should take them too seriously, they are essentially creatures of convenience.

Access I have walked without challenge throughout the Lake District for a great many years, and most walkers will enjoy the same freedom, especially if they stick to orthodox lines of ascent. The exploration of the fells is something to be enjoyed by everyone, and wandering freely across trackless ground is part of that pleasure. This general freedom however should not be interpreted as a licence to clamber over walls and fences indiscriminately causing damage, or to tramp through fields of crops. And to travel anywhere on the fells with a dog that is not held on a leash is inviting the wrath, and rightly so, of the men and women who earn a living in this delectable corner of England.

Table 1

The 600-metre mountains of the Lake District arranged in order of altitude with a minimum of 30 metres of re-ascent from all directions, including summits of sufficient topographical merit with less re-ascent.

	HEIGHT (m)	NAME	MAP REF.	VOLUME/ SECTION NUMBER	SECTION NAME
1	978	Scafell Pike	215072	1/7	Scafells
2	964	Scafell	207065	1/7	Scafells
3	950	Helvellyn	342151	2/4	Helvellyn
4	935	Ill Crag	223073	1/7	Scafells
5	934	Broad Crag	218076	1/7	Scafells
6	931	Skiddaw	260291	1/1	Skiddaw
7	925	Lower Man	337155	2/4	Helvellyn
8	910	Great End	227084	1/7	Scafells
9	902	Bowfell (Bow Fell)	245064	2/2	Langdale
10	899	Great Gable	211103	1/5	Great Gable
11	892	Pillar	171121	1/6	Pillar
12	891	Nethermost Pike	344142	2/4	Helvellyn
13	890	Catstye Cam (Catchedicam)	348158	2/4	Helvellyn
14	885	Esk Pike	237075	2/2	Langdale
15	883	Raise	343174	2/4	Helvellyn
16	873	Fairfield	359118	2/5	Fairfield
17	868	Blencathra (Saddleback)	323277	1/1	Blencathra
18	865	Little Man	267278	1/1	Skiddaw
19	863	Whiteside	338167	2/4	Helvellyn
20	859	Crinkle Crags (Long Top)	249049	2/2	Langdale
21	858	Dollywaggon Pike	346131	2/4	Helvellyn
22	857	Great Dodd	342206	2/3	Dodds
23	852	Grasmoor	175203	1/2	Grasmoor
24	843	Stybarrow Dodd	343189	2/3	Dodds
25	841	St. Sunday Crag	369134	2/5	Fairfield
26	841	Scoat Fell (Little Scoat Fell)	160114	1/6	Pillar
27	839	Crag Hill (Eel Crag)	193204	1/2	Coledale
28	834	Crinkle Crags – South Top	250046	2/2	Langdale
29	828	High Street (Racecourse Hill)	441110	2/6	High Street
30	828	Unnamed summit (Top of Black Crag)	166117	1/6	Pillar
31	826	Red Pike	165106	1/6	Pillar
32	822	Hart Crag	368113	2/5	Fairfield
33	819	Steeple	157117	1/6	Pillar

34	815	Shelter Crags	250053	2/2	Langdale
35	807	High Stile	170148	1/4	High Stile
36	803	Old Man of Coniston	273978	2/1	Coniston
37	802	Swirl How	273005	2/1	Coniston
38	802	Kirk Fell – South West Top	195105	1/5	Great Gable
39	802	High Raise	448134	2/6	High Street
40	801	Green Gable	215107	1/5	Great Gable
41	800c	Lingmell	209082	1/7	Scafells
42	797	Haycock	145107	1/6	Pillar
43	796	Brim Fell	271986	2/1	Coniston
44	795	Green Side (White Stones)	353187	2/3	Dodds
45	792	Dove Crag	375104	2/5	Fairfield
46	792	Rampsgill Head	443128	2/6	High Street
47	791	Grisedale Pike	198225	1/2	Coledale
48	787	Kirk Fell – North East Top	199107	1/5	Great Gable
49	785	Allen Crags	237085	2/2	Borrowdale
50	785	Great Carrs	270009	2/1	Coniston
51	784	Thornthwaite Crag	431100	2/6	High Street
52	783	Glaramara	246105	2/2	Borrowdale
53	780	Kidsty Pike	447126	2/6	High Street
54	778	Dow Crag	262978	2/1	Coniston
55	778	Harter Fell	460093	2/7	Mardale
56	776	Red Screes	396088	2/5	Fairfield
57	773	Sail	198203	1/2	Coledale
58	772	Wandope	188197	1/2	Grasmoor
59	770c	Grey Friar	260004	2/1	Coniston
60	770	Hopegill Head	186222	1/2	Coledale
61	766	Greatrigg Man (Great Rigg)	356104	2/5	Fairfield
62	763	Wetherlam	288011	2/1	Coniston
63	763	Stony Cove Pike (John Bell's Banner) (Caudale Moor)	418100	2/6	High Street
64	762	High Raise (High White Stones)	281095	2/2	Wythburn
65	762	Slight Side	210050	1/7	Scafells
66	760c	Mardale Ill Bell	448101	2/6	High Street
67	757	Ill Bell	436077	2/6	High Street
68	756	Hart Side	359197	2/3	Dodds
69	755	Red Pike	161155	1/4	High Stile
70	753	Dale Head	223153	1/3	Newlands
71	746	Carl Side	255281	1/1	Skiddaw
72	745	Black Sails	283007	2/1	Coniston
73	744	High Crag	181140	1/4	High Stile
74	740	Ulpha Fell (Little Stand) (Red How)	250034	2/2	Langdale
75	739	Unnamed summit (Grisedale Pike – South West Top)	194220	1/2	Coledale

76	739	The Knott	437127	2/6	High Street
77	737	Robinson	202169	1/3	Newlands
78	736	Harrison Stickle	282074	2/2	Langdale
79	736	Seat Sandal	344115	2/5	Fairfield
80	734	Long Side	248284	1/1	Skiddaw
81	730c	Sergeant Man	286089	2/2	Langdale
82	730	Kentmere Pike	465078	2/7	Longsleddale
83	727	Hindscarth	216165	1/3	Newlands
84	726	Ullscarf	291122	2/2	Wythburn
85	726	Clough Head	334225	2/3	Dodds
86	723	Thunacar Knott	279080	2/2	Langdale
87	720	Froswick	435085	2/6	High Street
88	719	Whiteside	175221	1/2	Coledale
89	718	Birkhouse Moor	364160	2/4	Helvellyn
90	715	Brandreth	215119	1/5	Great Gable
91	715	Lonscale Fell	285272	1/1	Skiddaw
92	713	Branstree	478100	2/7	Mardale
93	710	Knott	296330	1/1	Uldale and Caldbeck
94	709	Pike of Stickle (Pike o'Stickle)	274074	2/2	Langdale
95	706	Yoke	438067	2/6	High Street
96	705	Pike of Blisco (Pike o'Blisco)	271042	2/2	Langdale
97	703	Ladyside Pike	185227	1/2	Coledale
98	702	Bowscale Fell	333305	1/1	Blencathra
99	701	Cold Pike	263036 / 263035	2/2	Langdale
100	700c	Pavey Ark	284079	2/2	Langdale
101	699	Gray Crag	427117	2/6	High Street
102	697	Grey Knotts	217126	1/5	Great Gable
103	696	Rest Dodd	432136 / 432137	2/6	High Street
104	692	Seatallan	140084	1/6	Pillar
105	690c	Caw Fell	132110	1/6	Pillar
106	690c	Ullock Pike	244287	1/1	Skiddaw
107	690	Great Calva	291312	1/1	Uldale and Caldbeck
108	683	Bannerdale Crags	335290	1/1	Blencathra
109	675	Sheffield Pike	369182	2/3	Dodds
110	672	Scar Crags	208207	1/2	Coledale
111	672	Loadpot Hill	457181	2/6	High Street
112	670c	Wether Hill	456167	2/6	High Street
113	664	Tarn Crag	488078	2/7	Longsleddale
114	660	Carrock Fell	342336	1/1	Uldale and Caldbeck
115	660	Whiteless Pike	180190	1/2	Grasmoor
116	658	High Pike	319350	1/1	Uldale and Caldbeck
117	657	Place Fell	406169	2/6	High Street
118	655	Selside Pike	490111	2/7	Mardale

119	653	Harter Fell	219997	1/8	Dunnerdale
120	653	High Spy	234162	1/3	Newlands
121	651	Rossett Pike	249076	2/2	Langdale
122	651	Great Sca Fell	291339	1/1	Uldale and Caldbeck
123	648	Fleetwith Pike	206142	1/5	Great Gable
124	646	Base Brown	225115	1/5	Great Gable
125	642	Iron Crag	123119	1/6	Pillar
126	641	Dodd	164158	1/4	High Stile
127	638	Grey Crag (Sleddale Fell)	497072	2/7	Longsleddale
128	637	Causey Pike	219208	1/2	Coledale
129	637	Little Hart Crag	387100	2/5	Fairfield
130	633	Starling Dodd	142158	1/4	High Stile
131	632	Seathwaite Fell	227097	1/7	Scafells
132	632	Rosthwaite Fell (Cam Crag)	256114	2/2	Borrowdale
133	628	Rough Crag	454112	2/6	High Street
134	628	Yewbarrow	173085	1/6	Pillar
135	622	Birks	380144	2/5	Fairfield
136	621	Rydal Fell	357087	2/5	Fairfield
137	621	Walna Scar	258963	2/1	Coniston
138	618	Hartsop Dodd	411118	2/6	High Street
139	616	Great Borne (Herdus)	124164	1/4	High Stile
140	616	Great Lingy Hill	310340	1/1	Uldale and Caldbeck
141	616	Yewbarrow – North East Top (Stirrup Crag)	176092	1/6	Pillar
142	609	Illgill Head	169049	1/7	Scafells
143	608	High Seat	287180	2/2	Wythburn
144	608	White Maiden	253956 254957	2/1	Coniston
145	600	Black Combe	135855	1/8	Coastal Fells

Appendix to Table 1

Other named summits of over 600 metres, with less than 30 metres of re-ascent.

	Map Reference	Height (m)	Volume/ Section Number	Section Name	1:50 000 OS Map
Symonds Knott*	208067	959	1/7	Scafells	89/90
High Crag	343137	884	2/4	Helvellyn	90
Gategill Fell	318273	851	1/1	Blencathra	90
Atkinson Pike* (Foule Crag)	324283	845	1/1	Blencathra	90
Cofa Pike	359121	820c	2/5	Fairfield	90
Blease Fell	312270	804	1/1	Blencathra	90

Great Scoat Fell*	154112	802	1/6	Pillar	89
Watson's Dodd	336196	789	2/3	Dodds	90
Pen*	220069	768	1/7	Scafells	89/90
Sand Hill	187219	756	1/2	Coledale	89/90
Low Raise	456137	754	2/6	High Street	90
Caudale Moor (Caudale Head)	413101	750c	2/6	High Street	90
Buck Pike	263972	744	2/1	Coniston	96/97
Round How	219081	741	1/7	Scafells	89/90
Little Gowder Crag	140110	733	1/6	Pillar	89
Red Crag	450152	711	2/6	High Street	90
Great Knott	259042	696	2/2	Langdale	89/90
Little Carrs	270015	692	2/1	Coniston	89/90
Scales Fell	332279	682	1/1	Blencathra	90
Unnamed summit (Branstree)	488103	673	2/7	Mardale	90
Bakestall	266307	673	1/1	Skiddaw	89/90
Loft Crag*	277072	670c	2/2	Langdale	89/90
Brown Pike	261966	670c	2/1	Coniston	96/97
Sale How	276286	666	1/1	Skiddaw	89/90
Adam Seat	471091	664	2/7	Mardale	90
Calfhow Pike	331211	660c	2/3	Dodds	90
Coldbarrow Fell (Low Saddle)	288133	656	2/2	Wythburn	89/90
Tongue Head	241080	656	2/2	Langdale	89/90
Middle Dodd	397096	654	2/5	Fairfield	90
Snarker Pike	391075	644	2/5	Fairfield	90
Little Calva	282315	642	1/1	Uldale and Caldbeck	89/90
Harrop Pike	501078	637	2/7	Longsleddale	90
Hobcarton End	195235	634	1/2	Coledale	89/90
Honister Crag (Black Star*)	212142	633	1/5	Great Gable	89/90
Little Sca Fell*	289342	633	1/1	Uldale and Caldbeck	89/90
Looking Stead	186118	627	1/6	Pillar	89/90
Coomb Height	311327	627	1/1	Uldale and Caldbeck	90
Hare Stones*	315344	627	1/1	Uldale and Caldbeck	90
Drygill Head*	318342	622	1/1	Uldale and Caldbeck	89/90
Heron Pike	356083	612	2/5	Fairfield	90
Black Brow	384101	610c	2/5	Fairfield	90
Brown Crag	327177	610	2/4	Helvellyn	90
Miton Hill	329341	607	1/1	Uldale and Caldbeck	90
Yewbarrow – South West Top (Long Crag)	172083	606	1/6	Pillar	89/90
Buck Pike*	253077	606	2/2	Langdale	89/90
Round Knott	334337	603	1/1	Uldale and Caldbeck	90
Little Lingy Hill*	302334	600	1/1	Uldale and Caldbeck	90

* Denotes that the summit is not named on the 1:50000 map.

Section 1 – Skiddaw, Blencathra and the Uldale and Caldbeck Fells

	MAP REFERENCE	HEIGHT (m)	OS 1:50 000 MAP
Skiddaw			
Skiddaw	261291	931	89/90
Little Man	266278	865	89/90
Carl Side	255281	746	89/90
Long Side	248284	734	89/90
Lonscale Fell	285272	715	89/90
Ullock Pike	244287	690c	89/90
Blencathra			
Blencathra (Saddleback)	323277	868	90
Bowscale Fell	333305	702	90
Bannerdale Crags	335290	683	90
Souther Fell	354291	522	90
The Uldale and Caldbeck Fells			
Knott	296330	710	89/90
Great Calva	291312	690	89/90
Carrock Fell	341336	660c	90
High Pike	319350	658	90
Great Sca Fell	291339	651	89/90
Great Lingy Hill	310340	616	90

ROUTES

1.1 Skiddaw and Little Man from Keswick
1.2 Lonscale Fell from Keswick
1.3 Carl Side and Skiddaw by Longside Edge
1.4 Carl Side from Millbeck
1.5 Blease Fell
1.6 Gategill Fell
1.7 Hall's Fell ridge
1.8 Doddick Fell
1.9 Scales Fell
1.10 Sharp Edge
1.11 Bannerdale Crags from Mungrisdale
1.12 Bowscale Fell from Mungrisdale

It isn't difficult to understand how natural and apt was the poet Southey's reference to "My neighbour Skiddaw", for nowhere in Britain does a mountain so dominate a town as Skiddaw does Keswick. Turn virtually any corner in this charming town, and the mountain is there looming above you, intimidating, frowning on the bustling ways of men like a benevolent old giant. And 'old' is an apposite description here, for the rocks of Skiddaw – Skiddaw Slate – are by far the most ancient in the Lake District.

Yet for all its size and height, Skiddaw is a mountain which on a fine summer's day gives itself up easily to the hill-walker, offering little in the way of challenge to experienced walkers, save by the ascent along Longside Edge or over Carl Side from Millbeck. For this reason it is regarded by some more blasé walkers as a bit of a bore, but it continues to attract even the most novice hill-walker to scale its heights, giving a taste of mountaineering in return for a little effort.

By comparison Blencathra – known in the past also as Linthwaite Pike, Threlkeld Fell, Blencrater and Blenkarthur, and in the present by the wholly unimaginative Saddleback – is a far superior mountain despite its lesser height. On Blencathra you could tramp for a whole week, ascending to its neat summit cairn by a different route every day, and each of them, certainly from the south, impressive, rugged and entertaining. Only from the north, from the silent area known as 'Back o'Skidda'', does the mountain lose its appeal. Here the scarred and rocky southern face gives way to the grassy spread of

Mungrisdale Common and the heather-cloaked peak of Great Calva lying across the wide valley of the River Caldew.

In this bleak area beyond the enormous barrier formed by Skiddaw and Blencathra, a barrier emphasised by Bassenthwaite Lake, the Vale of Keswick and the River Glenderamackin and only breached by the fault line now occupied by Glenderaterra Beck, lies the vast wilderness of Skiddaw Forest and the Uldale and Caldbeck Fells. This is a wild, intriguing place, unique in Lakeland; wide, smooth-sided valleys, broad grass and heather uplands, and boggy flats more typical of the Pennines than of Lakeland. A true forest of olden time, but more latterly a 'forest' in the sense of a sporting reserve, it is now virtually a treeless landscape, and completely uncultivated. It is an area demanding excellent map and compass technique, especially in misty conditions.

The moorland basin itself, draining the headstreams of the River Caldew, and the land to the west of the Caldew, was developed during the nineteenth century as a grouse moor, and so managed until as recently as the 1950s. By contrast the land to the east – Blencathra to Bowscale Fell – has a history of management for sheep farming, and was never part of the grouse moor. As a result, the hills of the west are heather-covered, while those to the east are more predominantly grass.

In the middle of the whole area, surrounded by the only substantial stand of trees left here, is a row of cottages, Skiddaw House (288291), all that remains to tell of the hardships and hardiness of Lakeland shepherds. It is now used as an open bothy (Border Bothies Association) and an outdoor pursuits centre.

These unvisited northern fells were also the hunting territory of John Peel, born in Caldbeck in 1776 and celebrated in song in his own lifetime by his friend John Woodcock Graves. Compared to the high summits on their southern edge, these northern fells are but minor bumps, but what a Godsend on a bank holiday or at the

Skiddaw from the top of Foule Crag (Atkinson Pike).

height of the summer when everywhere else is thick with less adventurous souls. You can keep Skiddaw – though I won't disown Blencathra – but these quiet, unassuming, isolated hills even on a wet day are a corner of Heaven set aside for lovers of the wind, the moors, and the haunting call of curlew overhead.

Route 1.1 Skiddaw and Little Man from Keswick "The ascent of Skiddaw is easy, even for ladies, who have only to sit their ponies to find themselves at the top, after a ride of six miles." Such was the Victorian view of Harriet Martineau, who went on to qualify her remarks by stressing the importance of taking a guide. Leigh's *Guide to the Lakes*, published in 1840, comments that the excursion is "very fatiguing", and likewise regards a guide as "absolutely necessary, as the mountain is frequently visited by sudden mists. Great coats and cloaks will be found very pleasant companions at the summit of the mountain, where the air is remarkably keen. The party should also be provided with sandwiches and brandy, to recruit their strength previous to the descent." The consumption of alcohol on mountains seems to have been an established part of the Lakeland scene in the past, and there is evidence that one party at least (embracing the Wordsworth and Southey families, and in the company of James Boswell, son of the biographer), who had climbed Skiddaw to light a bonfire in celebration of the victory at Waterloo, came down albeit safely but definitely merrier for Wordsworth's having accidentally kicked over the water container, thereby compelling everyone to drink neat rum to assuage their thirst – a likely story!

Skiddaw, the sixth highest summit in Lakeland, is indeed easily ascended, and the track to its stony summit so well blazed as to cause no difficulties to an attentive mind, even in mist. Nor is it especially difficult underfoot

Few walkers, I suspect, would instantly recognise this view of Skiddaw from the secluded valley of Southerndale.

– while preparing this book I spent some of the ascent in the company of one young man who walked up barefoot – no mean feet, so to speak!

I prefer the ascent to start in Keswick town centre, though it can be shortened by driving to the top of Gale Road (281253). This however avoids the pleasant ascent around the base of Skiddaw's lowly minion, Latrigg, often sufficient reward in itself for walkers with only a little time or inclination available.

From the town centre car park make for Fitz Park by the road which leads past the Gas Showrooms, and follow a signed road left and then right to the bridge across the River Greta and so into the park. Cross the park diagonally left (avoiding the football pitch) to an iron gate at the start of a fenced pathway leading in turn to another gate near the abutments of an old railway bridge. Turn right, and continue along the road for a few hundred metres to Spoony Green Lane. Now continue along the obvious track, climbing most of the time until the metalled road-way (the top of Gale Road) is reached. Move right to a stile (there are actually two, one obviously leading on to Latrigg, and the other giving on to a narrow, fenced pathway), and follow the fenced path to a small monu-ment to the memory of the Hawells, Skiddaw shepherds noted for their skill in breeding the ubiquitous Herdwick sheep of Lakeland. The early part of this ascent, skirting Latrigg and passing through and along the edge of small afforested areas is especially pleasing; the trees are haven for many species of bird, and as you advance so too does the prospect of the valley below and the mass of Skiddaw and its acolytes above.

Beyond the monument Jenkin Hill looms massively, and on a clear day the sight of walkers plodding wearily up this long incline is a daunting one. But that is all it is, a weary plod, until first Little Man and then the long, grey ridge of Skiddaw itself come into view.

Near the top of Jenkin Hill, which possesses a summit cairn (at 273275), there is a fence, and from here you can

follow a fence-line upwards to ascend to the top of Little Man by a well-worn path, continuing easily over the summit to regain the main track south east of Skiddaw's south summit. For Skiddaw, ignore this diversion and continue around Little Man before ascending the broad, stony shoulder to the south summit, from where a short, rocky journey northwards brings you to the trig and impoverished shelter on the summit.

DISTANCE: 7.3 kilometres (4.5 miles)
ASCENT: 830 metres (2725 feet)

The view from the summit of Skiddaw northwards is astonishing, taking in the whole of the Solway Firth and the lands of Dumfries and Kirkcudbrightshire over 40 kilometres (27 miles) distant; eastwards lie the low (by comparison) northern fells of the Skiddaw Forest, the long, grassy posterior of Blencathra, and the far off hills of the High Street range. The view south and west however, across the interior of Lakeland, is better from Little Man or Carl Side.

Route 1.2 Lonscale Fell from Keswick For all its graceful outline and blatantly impressive east face, Lonscale Fell is only infrequently visited; walkers who are prepared to toil to the summit of Skiddaw appear reluctant to extend their day to take in Lonscale. Even on an August Bank Holiday, other walkers can be seen from a distance, and you don't walk on their heels, as you would have to up Skiddaw. The summit of the fell, surprisingly, is a large flat plateau, almost big enough to accommodate a football pitch, followed by a short dip before the east peak is reached.

▲ *Traversing the marshy ground between Lonscale Fell and Jenkin Hill en route to distant Skiddaw.*

◀ *The summit of Skiddaw.*

The easiest approach is to use Route 1.1 to a point, about three-quarters of the way up the steep slope of Jenkin Hill, where the fence-line followed thus far deviates to the right. Stay with the fence, and in a short distance take to a narrow path leading to the col between Little Man to the left, and Lonscale Fell. Pass through a gate and turn right, ascending easily to the summit of the fell, marked by a modest cairn.

DISTANCE: 5.4 kilometres (3.4 miles)
ASCENT: 610 metres (2000 feet)

No visit to Lonscale Fell would be complete without the short extension to the east peak where you will encounter perhaps the most dramatic example of everything that is inspiring about hill-walking, in the chasm of the Glenderaterra at your feet.

Route 1.3 Carl Side and Skiddaw by Longside Edge

This variant route to Skiddaw is far superior to the customary way over Jenkin Hill, having a start in a region

The alluvial link between Bassenthwaite Lake and Derwentwater.

of the Lake District neglected by most walkers, and offering superb views over Bassenthwaite Lake to the Grisedale hills, the low fells around Lord's Seat, and across the arable farm land that stretches northwards to the Solway Firth. The ascent starts over the knobbly summit of Ullock Pike before moving easily to Longside and Carl Side, after which (though the continuation is by no means obligatory, Carl Side being sufficient objective in itself) there is a strenuous grind to the south summit of Skiddaw.

Start over a stile at 236310 (near which there is room to park a few cars); this is along the minor road to Orthwaite, and is a paradise at the right time of year for walkers interested in wild flowers. Cross the stile and follow a Land-Rover track across the field, making for another stile in the top left corner. From here follow an obvious route to the intake wall and another stile on which a blue arrow directs you to an excellent track leading into the unsuspected and beautiful recesses of Southerndale.

The track leads to yet another stile and later crosses Southerndale Beck by a bridge. Just before the bridge start to move diagonally right, using sheep tracks or a vague pedestrian path, to ascend easily to the ridge rising ahead to the dark, symmetrical peaks of Ullock Pike. The slopes of Longside Edge, along which lie the summits of Longside and Carl Side, fall gracefully into Southerndale, while to the left rise the screes of Skiddaw. Once on the ridge to Ullock Pike follow the path up a series of steps to what appears from below to be the summit of the fell, but, in spite of the cairn sprouting from its top, the true summit, with a dismal, flattened cairn, lies a few strides further on.

DISTANCE: 2.9 kilometres (1.8 miles)
ASCENT: 540 metres (1770 feet)

Southerndale, a delightful valley hidden away between Skiddaw and the fine ridge of Longside Edge. The double-topped summit is Ullock Pike. ▶

The ridge beneath Ullock Pike may also be reached by a steep path leaving the A591 immediately before the Ravenstone Hotel, at 236296. The path starts over a stile and ascends along the northern edge of Thornthwaite Forest (named 'Dodd Wood' on the 1:50 000 map) as far as a gate where it breaks out on to the open hillside. Follow the path climbing left and uphill until it curves right to join the ridge. This route is shorter, but lacks the interest and scenery of Southerndale.

The continuation from the heather and bilberry-carpeted summits of Ullock Pike to Longside has a lofty air about it and, despite its comparative remoteness from the centre of things, offers some interesting views of higher summits to the south. The summit of Longside, a couple of strides off the path, is marked by a small cairn.

DISTANCE: 0.5 kilometres (0.3 miles)
ASCENT: 60 metres (195 feet)

From Longside the path aims for Skiddaw rather than Carl Side, and walkers making for Carl Side should therefore take care in mist not to be led astray. Stay on the main path to the col with Skiddaw, on which a small pond, Carlside Tarn, gathers, and then turn right abruptly to gain a path rising to the large cairn on the top of Carl Side. In clear conditions you can leave the main path before the col and make straight for the summit cairn.

The view from Carl Side is not the best in the Lake District by any means, the mountain being dwarfed by its immediate and higher neighbours, but the prospect of the mountains at the head of Borrowdale, over the vast expanse of Derwentwater, is sufficiently rewarding to make Carl Side an acceptable terminus of a short day's walk.

DISTANCE: 0.75 kilometres (0.5 miles)
ASCENT: 50 metres (165 feet)

The continuation to Skiddaw presents no great difficulties, other perhaps than shortage of breath, and after much clattering on screes of broken slate, leads directly to the south summit where Route 1.1 is joined.

DISTANCE: 1.25 kilometres (1 mile)
ASCENT: 215 metres (705 feet)

In the event of sudden bad weather the quickest way back to the start is by a steep but not unduly fearsome descent from Carlside col directly into Southerndale to gain an excellent track leading back to the bridge mentioned earlier. Conversely you can ascend by this enclosed route, but I can't imagine why you would want to!

Route 1.4 Carl Side from Millbeck I suggested in Route 1.3 that Carl Side was sufficient objective in itself in spite of the opportunity it affords to continue to Skiddaw; that sentiment is if anything underlined by the pleasure you can gain from the ascent of Carl Side from Millbeck. Even so, it would be misleading to imply that this route is less than strenuous – all the fun of it lies in the retrospective view, southwards, over Keswick and Derwentwater to the distant fells of central Lakeland.

Millbeck is a small village about 3 kilometres (1.9 miles) north of Keswick, and immediately at the foot of Carl Side. It is best approached by leaving the A591 at 253258 along the minor road to the village, and at the T-junction turning left to cross Mill Beck (not named on the 1:50000 map). In a short distance turn sharp right to reach a sign-posted path to Skiddaw. Follow the path, which soon breaks out on to open hillside, and continue, initially steeply, but easing later, directly to the summit, marked by a cairn. The start of this route in descent is also marked by cairns.

DISTANCE: 2.8 kilometres (1.75 miles)
ASCENT: 655 metres (2150 feet)

The continuation to Skiddaw lies north east, by a descending path leading to Carlside Tarn where it joins the path

Longside Edge, Skiddaw and Little Man.

from Longside Edge. There is a less distinct, less direct, ascent to Skiddaw's south summit a short distance right of the main track, and this is useful when the main route is crowded, but it is unremittingly steep.

Walkers who don't mind a bit of roadwork will find the ascent of Route 1.3 to Carl Side, followed by the descent to Millbeck, an especially pleasant experience.

Route 1.5 Blease Fell It must be said at the outset that Blease Fell is by far a better way off Blencathra than a way up it. There are no continuously clear paths to follow, nor for the most part does the terrain justify any.

1.5a From Threlkeld Start from the car park (318256) in Threlkeld village and follow a sign-posted path ('Blease' and 'Blencathra') into a narrow wooded gorge flanking Blease Gill. Cross the gill by a plank bridge and continue to a gate leading on to open hillside. Re-cross the gill, by

Blencathra and sunlit Sale How from the summit of Skiddaw.

boulder-hopping, wherever you feel you can safely do so. Continue on a vague grassy path alongside the true right bank of Blease Gill until you pass beyond enclosures on the left, and then simply make for and follow the obvious edge of the fell as it passes across the top of Knowe Crags.

DISTANCE: 1.8 kilometres (1.1 miles)
ASCENT: 615 metres (2015 feet)

1.5b From Blencathra Centre Formerly a sanatorium, the Blencathra Centre lies at the end of the minor road running west from Threlkeld village, beyond which runs a broad track curving eventually round into Glenderaterra and the sanctum, 'Back o' Skidda''. Where the roadway ends, pass through a gate and either climb immediately right to gain a broad grassy path through bracken, or continue ahead for about eighty metres to the foot of the same grassy path and ascend from there. The path makes for a small quarry area, but turn left to continue climbing, just before the quarry is reached. Once clear of the bracken take the line of least resistance, making for the top of Knowe Crags, and from there continue easily to the top of the fell.

DISTANCE: 1.7 kilometres (1 mile)
ASCENT: 525 metres (1720 feet)

Continue to Blencathra's summit by following the escarpment edge, passing first over the top of Gategill Fell: there is a path all the way.

DISTANCE: 1.3 kilometres (0.8 miles)
ASCENT: 95 metres (310 feet)

Either line of ascent may be reversed without difficulty; Route 1.5a is easier, but only because Knowe Crags act as a sure guide in mist to start with, and Blease Gill is an easy target once you are below them.

Route 1.6 Gategill Fell Viewed from the village of Threlkeld, the broad base of Gategill Fell (sometimes 'Gate Ghyll') tapers to a rocky crown, Knott Halloo. Up to this point on the ascent the going is arduous, but the second half, amply recompensing the effort, is quite splendid.

Start from the car park in the village (318256), and follow the sign-posted path mentioned in Route 1.5a into a narrow, wooded gorge flanking Blease Gill. Continue to the gate giving on to the open hillside. Knott Halloo is prominent directly above, while the slopes of Blease Fell rise on the left.

Continue, following a wall, along the true left bank of Blease Gill, and ascend steadily to Knott Halloo where the ridge abruptly narrows; such difficulties as there remain on the rest of the ascent can easily be by-passed.

DISTANCE: 1.8 kilometres (1.1 miles)
ASCENT: 660 metres (2165 feet)

You can reach Blencathra's summit by following the path north east along the edge of the drop to Gate Gill.

DISTANCE: 0.6 kilometres (0.3 miles)
ASCENT: 35 metres (115 feet)

Route 1.7 Hall's Fell ridge   Taking its name from Threlkeld Hall at its base, Hall's Fell ridge has everything a
hill-walker could wish for. It is the most direct confron-
tation with a mountain in the whole Lake District, it is
an exhilarating and energetic ascent with splendid views,
it forms near the top a sharp edge – known as Narrow
Edge – that affords pleasant scrambling and spices things
up a bit. And, most encouraging of all, it leads directly
to the summit. It is known to fell-runners, and for reasons
that soon become obvious, as 'Knee-wrecker Ridge'!

The ascent starts at Threlkeld village along a metalled
road on the right (324255), a short distance from the A66.
Follow the road, and opposite buildings on the right, turn
left on to a gravel track leading to Gategill farm. Continue
between farm buildings on a sign-posted path to a gate

*The saddle of Saddleback (Blencathra) is a familiar landmark for motorists
entering the Lake District along the A66 from Penrith.*

and a path running alongside Gate Gill. At the top of the path, where there is a seat for those who are already weary (and if you are, you had better turn back, right now!), pass through a gate and a few strides further on cross the gill to gain a steeply ascending path climbing through bracken on to the broad base of Hall's Fell ridge. This is where the hard work starts, but it isn't half as long as it feels at the time. Soon the angle eases, as Doddick Fell and Scales Fell come into view, but if you really want convincing how easy Hall's Fell is, take a look at Gategill Fell on your left!

Higher up the ridge, beyond the bilberries which in July and August can cause no end of delay, there is a good deal of rock, virtually all of it avoidable on good paths. The crest however provides an entertaining, scrambly route without undue difficulty in good conditions; but in winter this is an ascent of alpine proportions. And a very fine one, too!

DISTANCE: 2.5 kilometres (1.6 miles)
ASCENT: 720 metres (2360 feet)

Such is the popularity of Hall's Fell ridge that a good path now exists all the way to the summit, and prevents anyone from going astray in even the poorest visibility. The same does not hold good once you reach the summit, however. On a clear day the panorama is spectacular, and the continuation to adjoining ridges and fells obvious and alluring. But in bad conditions, while the rim of the southern escarpment of Blencathra acts as a good guide for Gategill Fell, Blease Fell, and Scales Fell (watch for two cairns about ten metres apart on the right of the path leading from the summit cairn), difficulty can be experienced in locating the top of Foule Crag, named Atkinson Pike, for walkers heading for Mungrisdale Common and Bannerdale Crags. Sharp Edge lies at the end of the path leading east from the summit, and while it is easy to follow, care is needed at the start of the descent over rock to the beginning of the edge proper.

The ridges of Blencathra are best viewed from the slopes of Clough Head: they are (l. to r.) Blease Fell, Gategill Fell, Hall's Fell, Doddick Fell
▲ *and Scales Fell.*

The semi-circular rising path through Mousthwaite Comb is the easiest way to Scales Fell or Sharp Edge. A steeper option leaves the comb lower down and follows the long shoulder of Scales Fell. ▲

Route 1.8 Doddick Fell The ascent of Blencathra by way of Doddick Fell is only surpassed by Hall's Fell ridge and Sharp Edge. It is an ideal alternative to both those routes when they are thronged with the summer multitudes of peak-baggers. Doddick Fell is for the connoisseur, the only note of demerit is its lack of a direct line to the summit plateau of the mountain, having to consort with Scales Fell for the final pull.

Start at Scales, near the White Horse Inn (343269), and walk along the main road in the direction of Keswick for a few hundred metres until at a small lay-by on the right between two cottages you can cross an adjacent area of open land to a gate (not always visible from the road when the grass is high). From the gate go left along the line of a wall until you meet Scaley Beck (not named on the 1:50000 map). Cross the beck and ascend directly to the start of Doddick Fell which will give you the finest view possible of the summit of Blencathra towering above Doddick Gill. The ridge before you requires no detailed description, the route is clear enough and in any event delineated by noticeable drops on both sides. Near the top, an alternative finish cuts right to the col with Scales Fell, but the direct route poses no problems. From the top of Doddick Fell ascend left on a good path to join the path from Sharp Edge only a short distance from the summit of Blencathra.

DISTANCE: 2.5 kilometres (1.6 miles)
ASCENT: 650 metres (2130 feet)

Route 1.9 Scales Fell This is the least physical ascent of Blencathra, and is neither especially rewarding nor blessed with much of interest en route, though it does afford a fine view into the corrie containing Scales Tarn,

Sunlight and shadows on the saddle of Saddleback (Blencathra) and Sharp Edge.

and offers, from the top of Doddick Fell, an imposing view of Blencathra's summit.

As for the ascent of Doddick Fell (Route 1.8), start at Scales, near the White Horse Inn (343269), and walk the short distance to the gate at the top of the area of open land adjacent to the main road. From the gate follow the conspicuous track heading right (north east) and rising across the lower slopes of Scales Fell. This later climbs steeply to gain the rim of Mousthwaite Comb, and then continues across the linking ridge between Scales Fell and Souther Fell to follow the line of the River Glenderamackin. (This forms an alternative, shorter start to Route 1.10.)

Where the path meets the linking ridge, or sooner if you think the going looks easy enough, you should ascend steeply left up the grassy, trackless shoulder of Scales Fell for almost a kilometre (0.6 miles) until you arrive on the ridge overlooking Scaley Beck (not named on the 1:50000 map, and not to be confused with Scales Beck, flowing from Scales Tarn, which isn't named either!). The ascent along the ridge, where a path now appears, is delightful; Scales Tarn and Sharp Edge are prominently in view to your right, while to your left a steep escarpment falls to Scaley Beck beyond which rises Doddick Fell, and beyond that, Hall's Fell ridge – the most direct of all the ascents of Blencathra.

Continue easily above the escarpment to the top of Doddick Fell – what a pity this fine ridge doesn't have its own distinctive summit to go with it! – and finally ascend, a little more steeply, to meet a good path leading left, to the summit.

DISTANCE: 3.6 kilometres (2.25 miles)
ASCENT: 650 metres (2130 feet)

In view of the relative ease with which you can ascend Scales Fell, it follows that this route is best reserved as a means of descent, when the only problem will be discovering where the path has gone to once you reach the southern

end of the ridge above Scaley Beck. You can continue directly ahead from this point, but a desperately steep descent awaits you. Better is a left turn (east) to make for the col with Souther Fell, before which you will intersect the good path around the rim of Mousthwaite Comb, and can follow it back to Scales.

Route 1.10 Sharp Edge This way to the summit of Blencathra is as rewarding and entertaining as any, and compares favourably with 'scrambly' ascents elsewhere in the Lake District. The route begins easily enough, ascending through the wide hollow of Mousthwaite Comb between the southern extremities of Scales Fell and Souther Fell, and later paralleling the course of the River Glenderamackin before ascending neatly into the corrie basin housing Scales Tarn, beneath the notched brow of Sharp Edge. Some walkers consider the longish approach to Scales Tarn dreary and unappetising, but I have always found this splendidly wild area quite the opposite, and relish the pull out of Mousthwaite Comb leaving behind ever-widening views of the Dodds, and the Helvellyn and High Street ranges and beyond, the sudden panorama northwards over Bannerdale Crags and Bowscale Fell, and the easy stroll to where Scales Beck tumbles to the Glenderamackin.

Take the minor road, sign-posted 'Souther Fell', just east of the White Horse Inn (343269) and follow it until you start to descend to the bridge across Comb Beck (not named on the 1:50 000 map). Here ascend left (sign-posted 'River Glenderamackin: Mungrisdale Common') to a stile, and continue along the edge of a field (frequently wet) to gain the conspicuous rising track curving round

The dark cliffs of Tarn Crags and Sharp Edge rise behind sunlit Brunt
▲ *Knott. The route to them passes in front of Brunt Knott.*

◄ *Profile of Sharp Edge (Blencathra).*

the upper section of Mousthwaite Comb. At the col head south west towards Scales Fell on a grassy track, but in case you should need to return this way in mist, note first the prominent track which from the col crosses the shoulder of Souther Fell; it is easy to mistake this track for the one used on the ascent, and it will lead you away from where you want to be (see Route 1.13 for details).

The path running with, but high above, the Glenderamackin can also be reached from Scales by a variant route using the start of the ascent of Scales Fell (Route 1.9); in fact it is a direct continuation of the path from Scales. Instead of turning upwards to gain the shoulder of Scales Fell, continue ahead towards the Glenderamackin where the grassy track coming from Mousthwaite Comb joins from the right.

Follow the path, with the Glenderamackin below you on the right, until it meets Scales Beck, and then cross

Sharp Edge and Scales Tarn.

the beck and ascend to Scales Tarn. It would take a hard soul not to be impressed by the setting of Scales Tarn, and a selfish one to deny oneself the luxury of a few moments' contemplation in this wild sanctum. Harriet Martineau wrote in 1855: "The tarn is so situated at the foot of a vast precipice, and so buried among crags, that the sun never reaches it, except through a crevice in early morning." It is understandable then why Scales Tarn long held a reputation for its capacity to reflect the stars at noonday, though early travellers, including one who was so overcome by the power of the scenery that he "wished to lose blood and return", were often disappointed in their anticipation. Another, unidentified early traveller descending from Blencathra's summit commented: "We descended steeply, first southward, and then in an easterly direction to the Tarn; a beautiful circular piece of transparent water, with a well-defined shore. Here we found ourselves engulphed in a basin of steeps, having Tarn Crag on the north, the rocks falling from Sharp Edge on the east, and on the west, the soft turf on which we had made our downward progress."

A rest here, then, to appreciate how our ancestors may have viewed the scene. But beware, the sheep hereabouts have long been accustomed to visitors, as they have on Blencathra's summit, and are familiar with all the intricacies of rucksacks and the delicacies they contain.

From the tarn ascend a steeply-rising path to gain the end of Sharp Edge. Ahead the Edge rises dramatically offering an airy challenge, though many of its finer points are lost against the backdrop of higher cliffs beyond. The route across the Edge is clear enough, and walkers with a good head for heights will enjoy sticking to the crest as much as possible. Less adventurous visitors can avoid most of the rock work by following a narrow path on the north side of the Edge. There is an awkward manoeuvre towards the end of the Edge, but it isn't really that much of a problem in good conditions, providing you are prepared to use your rear end if prudence so dictates.

The view down to the top of Doddick Fell, with Scales Fell beyond.

Personally, I find the long, slanting gully beyond Sharp Edge more difficult than the Edge itself, and in wet weather this requires care, particularly near the top where there is a tendency to relax concentration. In winter, however, when it is encrusted in hoar and the higher slabs and gully sheened in ice, Sharp Edge is a vastly different ball-game, and needs great care and considerable experience!

Once up Sharp Edge, follow a good path for the short walk to the summit cairn, passing en route the start of the descent to Scales Fell and Doddick Fell, marked by two cairns about ten metres apart.

DISTANCE: 4.5 kilometres (2.8 miles)
ASCENT: 655 metres (2150 feet)

Route 1.11 Bannerdale Crags from Mungrisdale The broken escarpment which gives this summit its name turns its back to virtually the whole of Lakeland, presenting its array of slaty buttresses and gullies, once the scene of lead-mining activity, to the east. It is, as a result, from

◀ *At grips with Sharp Edge (Blencathra).*

the east, from the quiet village of Mungrisdale, that the most rewarding ascents begin though there are other ways, up, over and around the mountain's posterior – if clambering about on posteriors is what appeals to you.

Start along the narrow lane marked by a telephone box (362304), and pass by Bannerdale Cottage to gain, through a gate, a rough track heading towards the pyramidal form of The Tongue – in fact an elongated spur descending from Bowscale Fell. Bannerdale Crags are seen rising to the left of The Tongue, and soon the track heads in that direction. The river on the left here is the Glenderamackin which rises on the watershed between Bannerdale Crags and the slopes rising to Foule Crag and Blencathra.

1.11a A short distance from the village the track dips to cross a stream (from the right) which joins the Glenderamackin, and just at this point an initially indistinct footpath goes left, staying with the river to a collapsed sheep-fold where Bannerdale Beck flows into the river. Here (351295), gain the ridge rising westwards (the east ridge of the mountain) over grass and bracken, and follow the ridge to the summit, gaining the broad summit plateau a short distance south east of a slate cairn. The broken crags on the final section of the ridge, though affording an interesting diversion for walkers adept at scrambling, can be avoided on their southern (left) side.
DISTANCE: 3.25 kilometres (2 miles)
ASCENT: 450 metres (1475 feet)

1.11b An easier alternative lies in staying with the broad track along the southern slope of The Tongue instead of

---

The three main southern ridges of Blencathra – Gategill, Hall's Fell, and
▲ *Doddick Fell – from Scales Fell.*

◄ *The view down Hall's Fell Ridge from the summit of Blencathra.*

with the Glenderamackin. The track rises easily enough and later forks indistinctly: the main track heads left into the upper reaches of the cove, Bannerdale, where once lead was mined, but a grassy ramp (marked by a small cairn) rises right and leads to a large cairn (335302) near the col between Bowscale Fell and Bannerdale Crags. From here a clear path rims above Bannerdale, finally rising easily to the summit cairn.

DISTANCE: 4.25 kilometres (2.7 miles)
ASCENT: 450 metres (1475 feet)

Note that the cairn on Bannerdale Crags does not mark the highest point; this lies a short distance west at 335290, and is unmarked.

Bannerdale Crags may also be ascended by following the Glenderamackin to its source on the col due west of the summit below Foule Crag. But this way, while easy, is enclosed, and is much better as a descent.

The continuation, roughly north, to Bowscale Fell is best accomplished (if you want to keep your feet dry) by returning along the track round the rim of Bannerdale to the top of the grassy ramp mentioned in Route 1.11b, and then heading north to the summit. The path east–west across the col is no real use here.

Route 1.12 Bowscale Fell from Mungrisdale The ascent of this summit from Mungrisdale village is unlikely to tax anyone unduly. Yet even the most experienced hill-walkers will find something in its simplicity and tranquillity to remind them what the wild fells are all about. Less experienced walkers will discover much in the way of serenity to encourage them further.

1.12a By Bannerdale Begin by taking Route 1.11b to the col between Bowscale Fell and Bannerdale Crags. The true col, i.e. the lowest point, lies a short way south in a morass of boggy ground and tussock grass, but the cairn where the grassy ramp across the slopes of The Tongue reaches the col is the main objective. From here a path continues westwards into the next valley, while the summit of Bowscale Fell almost immediately comes into view. A compass bearing on the summit, especially in poor visibility, will lead you there across trackless ground in a matter of minutes.

The summit is marked by a large stone shelter, while a cairn, lower in height, lies about 60 metres further to the north east.

DISTANCE: 3.5 kilometres (2.2 miles)
ASCENT: 470 metres (1540 feet)

Returning in mist, remember that the track east–west across the col is a sure guide back to the cairn on the rim of Bannerdale. Walkers continuing to Bannerdale Crags are advised to return first to this cairn, and then to follow the path round the rim of the valley below in preference to squelching across marginally higher ground a short distance west. The cairn on Bannerdale Crags does not mark the highest point (see Route 1.11).

DISTANCE: 2 kilometres (1.25 miles)
ASCENT: 55 metres (180 feet)

1.12b By the east ridge Walkers who don't mind steep starts to the day should ascend Bowscale Fell by its east ridge, a much more rewarding approach than Route 1.12a, and one which affords a view of the glacial basin in which reposes Bowscale Tarn, once a must with itinerant Victorians and the home, traditionally, of two undying fish, further immortalised in Wordsworth's poem 'Song at the Feast of Brougham Castle'.

Start from 364306 and ascend steeply through gorse, bracken and rocky outcrops to gain the ridge, along which lie a few minor bumps before the cairn and then the summit shelter are reached.

DISTANCE: 3 kilometres (1.9 miles)
ASCENT: 470 metres (1540 feet)

Up 1.12a and down 1.12b, with a short diversion to take

in Bannerdale Crags first, makes an easy round trip for a day, but take care on the final section of the descending east ridge to avoid broken crags.

Route 1.13 Souther Fell from Scales Souther Fell is the long, squat mound on the right, the first mountain encountered, as you enter the Lake District along the A66 from Penrith. It is far overshadowed by higher mountains beyond, and sits beneath the conspicuous saddle which gives Blencathra its other less imaginative name, Saddleback. The ascent of Souther Fell is a half day affair best left for a warm summer's day when everyone else is trogging up Scales Fell and Sharpe Edge to Blencathra. Only then is its featureless, grassy summit – a broad ridge – likely to have any appeal beyond curiosity.

The simplest route is to follow Route 1.10 to the col at the head of Mousthwaite Comb, and then simply to turn right to ascend over trackless tussock grass to gain higher ground, before moving left, roughly north east, over a number of minor bumps to the modest cairn made up of large boulders on the summit. Do not be misled by the prominent cairn with a post sticking from it which you will pass en route.

DISTANCE: 3 kilometres (1.9 miles)
ASCENT: 290 metres (950 feet)

There is however a more enjoyable route to the col, starting a little over half a kilometre further along the road from the White Horse Inn. Instead of turning left into Mousthwaite Comb, cross the bridge over Comb Beck, through a gate, and continue until about thirty

▲ *Gategill Fell from the summit of Blencathra.*

◄ *Gategill Fell and Blease Fell from the top of Blencathra.*

metres before the next gate. Here, just beside a small stream, ascend left on a grassy track, which meanders up the southern slopes of Souther Fell eventually to the col, where the route described above can be followed.

DISTANCE: 3.7 kilometres (2.3 miles)
ASCENT: 290 metres (950 feet)

There is nothing about Souther Fell (sometimes 'Soutra Fell') as a mountain to capture the imagination, but, reliably attested, there are ghosts, for this is the very home of superstition and romance. Harriet Martineau tells the tale: "This Souter, or Soutra Fell, is the mountain on which ghosts appeared in myriads, at intervals during ten years of the last century – presenting precisely the same appearance to twenty-six chosen witnesses, and to all the inhabitants of all the cottages within view of the mountain; and for a space of two hours and a-half at one time – the spectral show being then closed by darkness."

The story begins on Midsummer Eve in 1735, when a farm-servant saw the whole of the eastern side of the mountain covered with marching troops coming from an eminence at the north end of the mountain and disappearing on the summit. Predictably, when he told his story "he was insulted on all hands". Two years later, also on Midsummer Eve, the farmer himself saw men on the summit apparently following their horses, but when he looked again a few minutes later, they were mounted and followed by "an interminable array of troops, five abreast, marching from the eminence and over the cleft, as before". Now it was the farmer's turn to be insulted! So, on Midsummer Eve "of the fearful 1745" – alluding to the Scottish rebellion – the farmer, a Mr. Lancaster, expressly invited twenty-six people to witness the occurrence. "Carriages were now interspersed with the troops; and every body knew that no carriages ever had been, or could be, on the summit of Souter Fell. The multitude was beyond imagination; for the troops filled a space of half-a-mile, and marched quickly until night hid them, – still marching. There was nothing vaporous or indistinct about the appearance of these spectres. So real did they seem that some of the people went up, the next morning, to look for the hoof-marks of the horses; and awful it was to them to find not one foot-print on heather or grass." Everything the witnesses saw was attested by them before a magistrate, when it also came out that two other people had seen the same thing in 1743, but had kept quiet about it once they had seen how their neighbours had been ridiculed.

By way of explanation the editor of the *Lonsdale Magazine* reported that it was discovered that on Midsummer Eve of 1745, the Scottish rebels were "exercising on the western coast of Scotland, whose movements had been reflected by some transparent vapour, similar to the Fata Morgana". That may have accounted for 1745, but what of the earlier years? Once the tale was out, and blessed with a certain degree of respectability, more tales emerged; spectral armies having been seen in Leicestershire in 1707, and over the summit of Helvellyn on the eve of the battle of Marston Moor in 1644. The summit of Souther Fell is still a chilling spot more than two hundred years later; happy ghost hunting!

Route 1.14 Coomb Height and Knott from Mosedale

Coomb Height is a minor bump in the middle of the long, descending east ridge of Knott. It squats to the east of a boggy depression guarding the final slopes of Knott, but most of the wet ground can be by-passed on the right where an indistinct path ascends to the ridge from Great Lingy Hill.

Start along the road from Mosedale, sign-posted 'Swineside' (358324), and continue to the vicinity of the Carrock Mine. Here, where Grainsgill Beck joins the Caldew, cross the beck and immediately start climbing steeply on a narrow path through bracken and heather up the shoulder of Coomb Height. Just after the angle of ascent eases a curious ditch is encountered. It is an artificial gully – a 'hush' – which served the mine, and is loose and unstable. In no circumstances should this be used either in ascent or descent. The summit of Coomb Height is marked by a small cairn.

DISTANCE: 4.7 kilometres (2.9 miles)
ASCENT: 405 metres (1330 feet)

Continue easily to Knott, avoiding the boggy ground if possible, up slopes of short grass, to a bald, featureless plateau that demands great care in mist even to retrace your steps. This is no place to rely on instinct: these innocuous-looking fells are confusing and dangerous if you can't see clearly where you are going. The only feature of Knott, apart from its ability to accommodate a football pitch, is its summit cairn.

DISTANCE: 1.5 kilometres (0.9 miles)
ASCENT: 95 metres (310 feet)

Route 1.15 Knott, Great Calva and Great Sca Fell from Orthwaite Knott is the highest summit of the Uldale and Caldbeck Fells, almost five kilometres (over three miles) from end to end including the minor summit, Coomb Height and the broad spur, Burn Tod (not a summit, though the 1:50 000 map suggests some re-ascent). In good weather it is excellent walking country, wet in places, but all of them avoidable, though the same cannot be said of the linking ground between Knott and Great Sca Fell. The ascent from Orthwaite of both mountains, plus many of the lower summits in this area, and including Great Calva, is a splendid day's walking.

Start along the bridleway, initially a farm access road (sign-posted 'Brocklecrag'), from 253336, and continue to a second bridleway sign at a point where a rising grass track, left, leaves the farm access road. While the farm access road is a better surface, easy to follow and takes you past the imposing quartz outcrop of Brocklecrag, the bridleway across the lower slops of Great Cockup gives a much better view of the surrounding country-side and avoids some of the marshy ground just after Brocklecrag.

Follow the bridleway, crossing a small ridge before descending towards the meeting of gills west of Burn Tod, where the continuation of the farm access road finally rejoins, having had to tackle some marshy ground en route. Once across Burntod Gill (not named on the 1:50 000 map) which flows from near the summit of Great Sca Fell, continue on a grassy path across the southern slopes of Burn Tod to gain the col between Great Calva and Knott, taking care near the top of the valley where there is an area of loose scree.

For Great Calva ascend, right, from the col (there is a faint path but it takes you across very wet ground), and then head south until you meet an old fence-line which can be followed, left, to the summit.

DISTANCE: 5.6 kilometres (3.5 miles)
ASCENT: 455 metres (1490 feet)

The summit of Blencathra, viewed from the top of Gategill Fell.

For Knott, ascend left from the col up grassy slopes that are in the main trackless and featureless, and which require care in misty conditions. The summit of Knott is a large plateau, and the highest point marked by a forlorn cairn.

DISTANCE: 5.2 kilometres (3.25 miles)
ASCENT: 475 metres (1560 feet)

Walkers making for Great Sca Fell first, which in spite of its name bears no comparison of any description with that other Scafell, need not use the Burn Tod approach. Instead follow Burntod Gill to a point where you can easily ascend to the col between Great Sca Fell and Meal Fell, and from there pick up a narrow, slanting grassy path cutting across the face of Great Sca Fell to the col with Little Sca Fell (289342 – not named on the 1:50000 map; its summit is marked by a large cairn and a shallow depression around which a few stones help create a wind-break). The summit of Great Sca Fell lies a short distance south of the col, and is marked by a modest cairn.

DISTANCE: 4.8 kilometres (3 miles)
ASCENT: 410 metres (1345 feet)

Perhaps the finest way by far of combining all these lonely fells is to ascend Great Calva by Route 1.16, and to continue from there to Knott, Great and Little Sca Fell, then descending, by the slanting grassy path, to Meal Fell, crossing Trusmadoor (a curious natural pass through the hills) on to Great Cockup, the ridge of which can be followed virtually all the way back to the road at Orthwaite.

Route 1.16 Great Calva by Dash Beck Although Great Calva lies at the very centre of a massive mountain region, I doubt if it receives one visitor for every thousand that tramp to the summit of nearby Skiddaw. In some ways that is a blessing, because Great Calva is a place for meditation rather than mass visitation. Travellers along the A66 between Penrith and Keswick who chance to gaze northwards through the gap between Blease Fell at the western end of Blencathra, and Lonscale Fell, will see Great Calva, a purple pyramid, positioned perfectly at the very point where the immense down-sweeping slopes of the two guardians of the sanctum known as 'Back o' Skidda'' meet. To my eye this alluring glimpse is irresistible, yet few walkers seem to take the trouble to find out how to get to Calva. The mountain has another attraction that is only obvious from its summit; it lies at the northern end of a massive fault line extending southwards through Glenderaterra, the Vale of Thirlmere, Grasmere, the Rothay valley and the whole length of Windermere lake. And the view you get of this as far as Dunmail Raise is terrific.

The finest approach to Great Calva uses the old supply road (a public bridleway) leading to Skiddaw House. Start from 249323 along the road (sign-posted 'Threlkeld and Skiddaw House via Dash Falls') which leads initially to Dash Farm. At 262320 the metalled road dips left to the farm, but a stone marker points the way to Dash Falls (shown on the 1:50 000 map as Whitewater Dash), not that this splendid cataract needs any pointer. The supply road passes beneath the imposing Dead Crags (better seen from Great Cockup to the north), before moving left to the top of the falls. In a short distance cross an attractive stone bridge spanning Dash Beck, and continue ascending on a clear path. You can if you wish continue all the way to Skiddaw House (now an Outdoor Pursuits Centre and a bothy) before doubling back to ascend the heathery slopes of Great Calva.

More direct is to follow the track until it reaches its highest point (not far beyond Dash Falls), and then to ascend steeply left to the spot height 614 on the minor summit, Little Calva. The spot height is not the summit of Little Calva, but it is a convenient place to rest for a while to take in the graceful lines of Skiddaw and the rugged Dead Crags. A short distance east from the spot

height, which is marked by a large cairn that from below lulls you into thinking the summit is at hand, a dilapidated fence-line is encountered, and this not only leads you over the summit of Little Calva (marked by another cairn a short distance from the fence) and on to Great Calva, but also takes you through some of the wettest terrain back o' Skidda'! The effort however is well worthwhile, for the final pull to the summit of Great Calva places you precisely at the northern summit (the southern summit, obviously lower, lies a short distance away), marked by a large cairn adorned by bits of old fencing and near to which is a superb windproof stone shelter, ideal for the quiet contemplation of this amazing wilderness of moorland.

DISTANCE: 4.8 kilometres (3 miles)
ASCENT: 475 metres (1560 feet)

In misty conditions a continuation to Knott is tricky and I do not advise it. If you must go, follow the old fence-line back towards Little Calva, but only as far as the point at which it first bends left. From here (287316) you must take a bearing on the narrow col just over one kilometre (0.6 miles) south west of Knott, and follow that, getting your feet wet again in the process. On a clear day you can move right a little from a direct line to gain some marginally better ground. The ascent from the col to the summit of Knott is quite featureless apart from one cairn in the middle of nowhere (which can be confusing in mist), and in poor conditions you will need good navigational ability to walk directly to the summit cairn.

DISTANCE: 2.6 kilometres (1.6 miles)
ASCENT: 145 metres (475 feet)

If you intend to move on from Knott, take into account that the summit is a totally bald plateau, higher than surrounding mountains (which cannot therefore be seen)

◄ *Hall's Fell ridge and the neat summit of Blencathra from Threlkeld.*

Carrock Fell, site of an ancient hill fort.

Bowscale Fell from the moorland to the north.

and the only feature on which is the summit cairn. Get any compass bearings exactly right before leaving the cairn behind; the whole of this inner region of Uldale and Caldbeck Fells can have you wandering around aimlessly if you fail to take care over navigation.

Route 1.17 Carrock Fell, High Pike and Great Lingy Hill from Mosedale In an area predominantly composed of Skiddaw Slates, Carrock Fell is an oddity. It is constructed of hard gabbro (the rock of which the Cuillins of Skye are made) and granophyre, giving the mountain complex a striking bulk which, far more resilient to the ravages of time, sets it high above the slates of the Caldew valley and the limestone plateau of Greystoke and Hutton Roof to the east. The effect is to produce one of the most sharply defined boundaries of the Lake District, and an area of great geological interest. There is also a suggestion that the erection of rocks on Carrock Fell is the work of the Devil, or a giant, or of Michael Scot, a famous reputed magician who is said to have retired in old age to the Cistercian abbey at Holm Cultram until his death in 1291.

Carrock Fell has other claims to fame; its summit is the

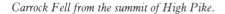

Carrock Fell from the summit of High Pike.

site of the largest known hillfort in Cumbria, considered to have been built during the Iron Age. The outlines of the fort are still clearly visible today, though the ramparts have been dismantled and scattered about in a manner which suggests other than the work of nature: the Romans have been blamed, but there is neither evidence nor supportable explanation to substantiate this. Carrock is also renowned for its mineral wealth, particularly for its output of wolfram (tungsten), a mineral found nowhere else in the Lake District. The mine, situated at the confluence of Brandy Gill (not named on the 1:50000 map) and Grainsgill Beck, opens and closes as world demand for tungsten fluctuates, and there is clear evidence that it has been operational in recent years.

To ascend then to this hill of substance, leave the village of Mosedale along the minor road to Swineside – this ultimately, as a pedestrian only, will take you all the way to Skiddaw House. Beyond the last house on the left there is an open stretch of ground before another wall is encountered. The ascent starts opposite this second wall. There is no path of any note, and walkers must choose their own line, generally heading diagonally left and sticking to sheep tracks through the gorse, heather and outcrops of scree (in many ways the scree is the easier ground) until the angle eases. The going initially is rough and steep, but once beyond this the summit comes into view across an intervening plateau of boggy ground, and is reached by a short bout of heather-bashing. The summit, inside the boundaries of the hillfort, is marked by a large cairn and a stone shelter.

DISTANCE: 2.4 kilometres (1.5 miles)
ASCENT: 445 metres (1460 feet)

The continuation to High Pike can be confusing in mist, but follows an indistinct path all the way, by-passing the lesser summit of Round Knott, but taking in Miton Hill (which has a nice cairn of large boulders) before descending to gain a Land-Rover track leading across

Drygill Head (318343 – not named on the 1:50000 map). On the ascent of Drygill Head leave the Land-Rover track for a narrower path making for High Pike, which in due course crosses a more substantial track to a shooting hut on Great Lingy Hill.

In bad weather a descent from the col between Miton Hill and Drygill Head, north east down Drygill Beck, or south via Brandy Gill (keep to the high ground above the gill, marked Longdale on the map) to Carrock Mine, will lead to safety. Shelter may also be found in the obvious man-made ravine just south of High Pike, which used to serve the Driggith mine lower down the fellside. The summit of High Pike is adorned by a large cairn, extending in the form of a shelter to encompass the trig point, while nearby, the only summit in the Lake District to possess one, is a stone bench to the memory of Mick Lewis, a young man who used to live in Nether Row a few kilometres to the north.

DISTANCE: 3 kilometres (1.9 miles)
ASCENT: 90 metres (295 feet)

Continue to Great Lingy Hill, a summit of no great consequence, by the excellent track to the shooting hut, noting however that the track does not cross the highest ground; you will have to hunt for the summit!
DISTANCE: 1.5 kilometres (0.9 miles)
ASCENT: 20 metres (65 feet)

A return to base may be made from the shooting hut, where the track ends, by following Grainsgill Beck to Carrock Mine where the metalled roadway to Mosedale is joined.

Route 1.18 High Pike from Nether Row, Caldbeck
High Pike is the most northerly of the Lakeland fells, and is probably visited more on that account than for any other merit, though it has an excellent view of the Border country and the Solway Firth. It is typical of the grassy,

moorland hills which make up the Caldbeck and Uldale Fells, its slopes are uniformly smooth and unlikely to tax even the least fit walker, and only watercourses and derelict mine workings offer any feature you can use for navigation.

Nether Row (324377), a scattered group of houses, lies due south of Caldbeck village, and is approached down a narrow country lane. When you reach the end of the metalled road surface the track ahead forks, right to the Potts Gill mine (320366), and left to the Sandbed mine (332363 – though neither mines are clearly named on the 1:50000 map). You can follow either of these routes without any difficulty, the way being sufficiently marked on the map and clear enough on the ground. If you take the Potts Gill route, watch for a faint path climbing left to the summit near Curly Job Well.

The Sandbed mine route is marked in black on the 1:50000 map (denoting that it is not a public right of way), but may be followed to the mine from where you can gain a prominent Land-Rover track, which follows the line of a footpath (shown on the map) at least as far as the shoulder of High Pike. You must ascend, right, from this path to reach the summit, which is marked by a trig point, a stone shelter cum cairn, and a stone seat.

DISTANCE: (via Potts Gill) 2.9 kilometres (1.8 miles); (via Sandbed) 4 kilometres (2.5 miles)

ASCENT: 400 metres (1310 feet)

The Land-Rover track, if you rejoin it, continues to a hut on Great Lingy Hill, and you can use it to 'bag' this inconsequential bump.

Section 2 – Whinlatter, Coledale and Grasmoor

	MAP REFERENCE	HEIGHT (m)	OS 1:50000 MAP
Whinlatter			
Lord's Seat	204266	552	89/90

Whinlatter (Top)	197249	525	89/90
Coledale			
Crag Hill (Eel Crag)	193204	839	89/90
Grisedale Pike	198225	791	89/90
Sail	198203	773	89/90
Hopegill Head	186222	770	89/90
Unnamed summit (Grisedale Pike)	194220	739	89/90
Whiteside	175221	719	89/90
Ladyside Pike	185227	703	89/90
Scar Crags	208207	672	89/90
Causey Pike	219208	637	89/90
Outside	211215	568	89/90
Grasmoor			
Grasmoor	175203	852	89/90
Wandope	188197	772	89/90
Whiteless Pike	180190	660	89/90
Ard Crags	207198	581	89/90
Knott Rigg	197188	556	89/90

ROUTES
2.1 Lord's Seat over Barf
2.2 Whinlatter
2.3 Grisedale Pike from Braithwaite
2.4 Crag Hill over Causey Pike, Scar Crags and Sail
2.5 Ladyside Pike and Hopegill Head
2.6 Whiteside and Hopegill Head from Lanthwaite Green
2.7 Grasmoor from Lanthwaite Green via Gasgale Gill
2.8 Grasmoor from Rannerdale via Lad Hows
2.9 Grasmoor from Braithwaite via Coledale Hause
2.10 Whiteless Pike and Wandope
2.11 Outside
2.12 Ard Crags and Knott Rigg

Like the Newlands Fells to the south, all the summits of the Whinlatter, Coledale and Grasmoor group are contained within the catchment area of the River Derwent which at Cockermouth is joined by the River Cocker for the remaining journey to the sea at Workington. The principal underlying rock is slate, and so all the fells have smooth profiles, making for easy walking, mostly on pleasant ground, though the fells central to the area, Grasmoor, Crag Hill and Grisedale Pike all have rugged aspects and fine, imposing situations. And, to enhance the area even further, many of the summits are linked by excellent ridges, notable amongst which are the long Causey Pike–Crag Hill ridge, the fine Whiteside–Hopegill Head ridge, easily linked with Grisedale Pike's own attendant ridges.

In a sense dissecting the area, nothing could contrast more than the two long valleys which rise to join at Coledale Hause (189213). Coledale itself, to the east, is smooth-sided and wider than the western Gasgale Gill where valleyside weathering and stream erosion have produced a remarkable landscape as rugged and grand as any to be found among rocks of the Borrowdale Volcanic Series, yet these are Skiddaw Slates.

The northern section, north of Whinlatter, is extensively afforested, and perhaps for that reason and the lower height of its summits is rather less favoured. But there are many more pleasant, short walks among them than I have described here, and the area will amply reward an occasional visit.

Route 2.1 Lord's Seat over Barf To walkers brought up on the rugged heights of the Scafells, Great Gable and the Langdales, the serene, delectable fells west of Bassenthwaite Lake, of which Lord's Seat is the highest, will come as a pleasant surprise. A hint of what lies in this quiet top left corner of the Lake District is gleaned as you drive over Whinlatter Pass and descend to High Lorton. But these grassy-topped summits are encircled about their feet with well-established Forestry Commission plantings, and the best overall views come from adjoining ranges, from Grisedale Pike and Skiddaw.

The ascent to Lord's Seat, once popular with the

The seldom visited summit of Whinlatter.

Victorians, starts from the car park opposite the Swan Hotel (220264). You will have to leave the A66 near Braithwaite to reach it. Pass through the trees on to a broad path which soon crosses Beckstones Gill (not named on the 1:50000 map), and, at a stile, gain a path, through gorse bushes, which ascends steeply along the edge of the Beckstones Plantation. The curiously-shaped lumps of rock, white-washed by locals, which have been named The Bishop and The Clerk and given undue prominence by the Ordnance Survey, contrast starkly with the dismally grey scree and rock slope on the right. This is an energetic start to the day, and climbs first to a small grassy platform before resuming the upwards grind, this time entering the forest by a zig-zag path which appears above a small rock outcrop. Follow the path until it joins a main forest road at a short level stretch. If subsequently descending by this route keep your eyes open for the small cairn marking the departure of the path from the main forest road, it can easily be missed.

Lord's Seat and the high moorland north of Whinlatter. ▶

As soon as the forest road starts to ascend again, watch for and take, a narrow descending path on the right, leading to a step stile. Beyond, across the upper part of Beckstones Gill, take a steeply rising path to the summit of Barf, which has been the massive bulk of hillside on your right as you ascended.

There is nothing to be said for omitting Barf from this ascent; a direct line, using forest trails, can be made for Lord's Seat, but this is best reserved for descent. The view of Bassenthwaite Lake and the Skiddaw massif from the top of Barf is quite remarkable, while the hitherto hidden hinterland is a splendid addition to one's walking repertoire.

Westwards from Barf little is seen except Lord's Seat, and the connecting ridge, criss-crossed by a series of paths and sheep tracks, and inhabited by red grouse, is a pleasure to walk. The summit of Lord's Seat requires a short pull to the two iron stanchions marking all that is left of a fence-line that once crossed the top.

DISTANCE: 2.4 kilometres (1.5 miles)
ASCENT: 450 metres (1475 feet)

If returning to the Swan Hotel aim first for the step stile across the nearby new fence-line and then for the bald prominence of Ullister Hill (209260 – not named on the 1:50 000 map), but before reaching it divert left, into the forest, by an intermittent path which will lead you eventually to the main forest roads. Take care, however, not to stray too far into the forest along these roads, and find that you have to back-track. If in doubt, descend in the direction of Barf at every opportunity.

The summit of Lord's Seat need not, however, signify an about turn. Beyond, again approached by splendidly easy walking, lies Broom Fell, its summit marked by a massive cairn, and further on, Graystones. All of this provides you with a delectable traverse to Lorton Vale, one well worth undertaking.

Route 2.2 Whinlatter Most walkers think of Whinlatter as the high motor pass from Braithwaite to Lorton Vale, and few I suspect appreciate that the rough northern wall of the pass culminates in an excellent grassy ridge, worthy of a short day's excursion.

Start from the top of the pass (204245) where the western boundary of Thornthwaite Forest meets the road. Here, enter the forest and ascend north eastwards by a broad forest road. As the road bends left, two side roads are encountered, the ground between them felled of trees. Take the second, higher side road and follow this to a turning area for forestry vehicles at its end. Continue a short distance through a few remaining boundary trees to a fence, beyond which lies the open hillside of Whinlatter. Cross the fence, taking care not to damage it, and ascend right until you gain the summit ridge.

Retrospective to Whiteside from near the summit of Hopegill Head.

The view northwards, over the valley containing Aiken Beck, to Lord's Seat and Broom Fell, is splendid, while the crest of Whinlatter undulates invitingly westwards to a cairned summit.

DISTANCE: 1.5 kilometres (0.9 miles)
ASCENT: 240 metres (785 feet)

Further on lies an apparently higher top, Brown How, which on the 1:50000 map bears the name, Whinlatter. But I assure you, the highest point of Whinlatter, some 8 metres (26 feet) higher than Brown How, lies at 197249.

Route 2.3 Grisedale Pike from Braithwaite The scars of the former direct ascent from Braithwaite to the start of the long ridge leading to Grisedale Pike were once

---

New Year's Day, 1986: the Whiteside–Hopegill Head ridge.

visible from beyond Blencathra along the A66, but conservation work is restoring the damaged ground to its former, bracken-clad condition. Walkers will in any event find the new start a less demanding option than the former.

Leave Braithwaite on the Whinlatter road, passing the original direct start, and continue to a small parking area from where a stepped path climbs away from the road. Follow this, and double back on it to rejoin the old route below the minor top, Kinn. Continue over Kinn on a good path, later climbing to join a higher ridge, Sleet How, at 207228. The path is flanked by low heather scrub, but soon leaves this behind for a final pull to the summit over slaty rock that can be nasty underfoot, especially in descent. This final section is badly eroded, and great care is needed at all times of the year. The

Grisedale Pike and its attendant unnamed summit.

summit is marked by a large cairn, and affords an excellent vista of the Solway Firth and the hills of Scotland.
DISTANCE: 3.5 kilometres (2.2 miles)
ASCENT: 680 metres (2230 feet)

The continuation to Hopegill Head follows a dilapidated wall over Grisedale Pike's second, unnamed summit (194220), from where walkers continuing to Coledale Hause (for Crag Hill or Grasmoor) can pick up a path, initially cairned, descending left. The route to Hopegill Head, which rises invitingly above the shattered face of Hobcarton Crag, continues with the fallen wall, until at the col it abruptly ends, and then takes a path along the rim of the cliffs, overlooking the Hobcarton and Swinside plantations to the north, for the final pull to the summit.
DISTANCE: 1.6 kilometres (1 mile)
ASCENT: 95 metres (310 feet)

Route 2.4 Crag Hill over Causey Pike, Scar Crags and Sail The knobbly summit of Causey Pike is a distinctive picture-postcard backdrop to the town of Keswick, and a helpful guide in locating other, less easily identified summits in the confusing array of mountain tops that encircle the town. For the hill-walker, Causey Pike is an energetic introduction to a superb mountain traverse which, extended to encompass Grisedale Pike (as recommended in Classic Walks 2 – the Braithwaite Horseshoe), affords a full day in the hills with never a dull moment.

Start from the bridge (233212) at Stonycroft, near the village of Stair, and follow the rising path across the flanks of Rowling End to the col between Rowling End and the cone of Causey Pike, as it now appears, towering above. Strong walkers can begin by ascending Rowling End. In either case a fair amount of energy will be expended early

The ascent to Hopegill Head from Ladyside Pike. ▶

in the day. The final pull to the summit of Causey Pike is rocky and delightful, and though it may require the use of hands near the top, need deter no one.

DISTANCE: 1.5 kilometres (0.9 miles)
ASCENT: 710 metres (2330 feet)

Once the summit is reached the long ridge to Crag Hill comes fully into view, undulating into the distance, with a fine panorama of mountains to the south, and shapely Grisedale Pike, one of the boundaries of the great medieval parish of Crosthwaite, rising to the north west above the intervening minor summit, Outerside.

Continue south of west along the ridge on a good path to the summit of the next mountain, Scar Crags – not to be confused with Scar Crag further on, the immense

Hobcarton End and Grisedale Pike from Swinside.

southern face of Crag Hill. The flat summit of Scar Crags, higher than Causey Pike but much less challenging, is marked by a large cairn.

DISTANCE: 1 kilometre (0.6 miles)
ASCENT: 55 metres (180 feet)

Cross a small grassy plateau before descending to the col with Sail. This col may be reached directly from Stonycroft by following a track, originally engineered to service a cobalt mine higher up the valley, along the true left bank of Stonycroft Gill (not named on the 1:50000 map) until you reach High Moss, by which time the path is less distinct, but can still be followed to the col.

The ascent of Sail, its summit marked by a small cairn, is uneventful, and is much less severe than it might seem as you descend from Scar Crags from where the perspective is shortened. The path does not pass over the highest point, and a short diversion is necessary as soon as you reach the neat summit plateau.

DISTANCE: 0.75 kilometres (0.5 miles)
ASCENT: 155 metres (510 feet)

The final section of this splendid ridge to Crag Hill, by far the most exhilarating, is woefully short. Descend from Sail to a dramatically narrow link with the higher summit, requiring care in winter conditions, before scampering easily up a narrow crest to the summit trig.

DISTANCE: 0.75 kilometres (0.5 miles)
ASCENT: 65 metres (210 feet)

Crag Hill, not the most imaginative name, is sometimes mistakenly called Eel Crag after the precipitous northern end of the mountain, which falls in a series of loose and broken cliffs to the valley of Coledale, and by a not much less risky slope to Coledale Hause. A descent of the former is out of the question, while a continuation in the latter direction by anyone undertaking the Braithwaite Horse-shoe is not recommended, in many places the ground is steep and unstable. A much safer alternative lies in heading west from the trig, as if making for Grasmoor, and at the col between the two mountains turning north along the right bank of upper Gasgale Gill to Coledale Hause. A descent to and from Coledale Hause, by a prominent and cairned path, passing Force Crag and its attendant mine into Coledale valley is the only safe retreat from Crag Hill in the event of bad weather (see Route 2.9 for details).

The continuation to Grisedale Pike from Coledale Hause is obvious enough, the route having become well trodden over the years, but take care approaching the hause not to stray too far down the much more prominent Coledale valley path.

Walkers with cars will find some advantage in parking in a small lay-by at 233222 and walking along the road to Stonycroft, returning to the lay-by from Braithwaite by the footpath to Braithwaite Lodge (233232 – not named on the 1:50000 map), near the small wood, Little Braithwaite. This is a very pleasant end to the day, and leads back to the road only a short distance from the lay-by.

Route 2.5 Ladyside Pike and Hopegill Head The long ridge extending northwards from Hopegill Head is a splendid walk, traversing the neat summit of Ladyside Pike. The route starts at two points along the Whinlatter road, and though the first calls for the expenditure of some energy in gaining the Swinside ridge it starts pleasantly enough through the Swinside Plantations, taking you into the bleak recesses of Hobcarton with an unfamiliar Grisedale Pike rising above them.

2.5a By Swinside Plantations Start at 186248 where a forest access road dips to cross Blaze Beck (not named on the 1:50000 map), and follow this to the edge of the plantations. Here turn left on a forest track, and continue, always ahead, until you escape from the plantations at a

The long grassy ridge of Ladyside Pike runs northwards to High Lorton. In the distance is the Solway Firth and the coastal hills of Scotland.

sheep pen. Above you rise the slopes of Swinside, dotted with the dead remains of old trees. Ascend steeply either by the forest line, or by another old fence a short distance further up the valley, to gain the grassy ridge. Once on the ridge follow a collapsed wall east of south to the cairn on the summit of Ladyside Pike.
DISTANCE: 2.8 kilometres (1.75 miles)
ASCENT: 450 metres (1475 feet)

2.5b From High Lorton This line of ascent is truly splendid, starting from a gate (176253), along a minor road which branches off from the Whinlatter Pass road. Unfortunately, the gate is marked 'Private', and there is no recognised right of way through the field that follows. It is therefore wise to seek consent to use this route, though a path crossing the field to another gate in the upper wall is obviously well used by walkers. In any event, take the greatest care, here as elsewhere, not to cause disturbance or distress to any animals grazing in the field or to damage any of the walls or gates.

Beyond the second gate the path continues through some minor outcrops to the summit of Swinside, near which a fence and an old wall need to be crossed, and then followed easily, and delightfully, to the top of Ladyside Pike.

DISTANCE: 2.8 kilometres (1.75 miles)
ASCENT: 445 metres (1460 feet)

The section linking Ladyside Pike and Hopegill Head is regrettably short. It is an exciting narrow arête culminating in a series of easy-angled slabs of bare rock, though the left edge should be kept at a safe distance. This is really good, and well worth repeating.

DISTANCE: 0.6 kilometres (0.4 miles)
ASCENT: 95 metres (310 feet)

Route 2.6 Whiteside and Hopegill Head from Lanthwaite Green There can be no better ascent of Whiteside than that which rises, almost forbiddingly, from the northern edge of Crummock Water at Lanthwaite Green. Viewed from the car park (158207) it promises a hard start to the day, having to tackle a minor top, Whin Ben, en route before getting to grips with Whiteside itself. It will come as no surprise to learn that the promise is fulfilled, a leg-buckling grind up a loose, slaty scree path will occupy you for the best part of an hour before you finally escape its clutches. But the ultimate reward is magnificent, amply repaying all the effort.

Cross the road from the car park and follow a broad green path, heading for the foot of Whin Ben. Here, where Gasgale Gill, descending from Coledale Hause, suddenly becomes Liza Beck, cross the stream by a wooden bridge and turn left to follow a path for a few metres until it bends right to start work on Whin Ben. From here on there is a relentless plod all the way to the top of Whiteside, but do as I do, and make a point of stopping frequently to admire the view and take photographs – the Loweswater Fells, Mellbreak prominent in the foreground, the domed shape of Red Pike off to the left and the ridge to High Stile and High Crag, the impressive broken face of Grasmoor End, the splendid, enclosed valley of Gasgale Gill at your feet, and, as finally you top Whin Ben, your first glimpse of the long ridge of Whiteside leading unerringly to the peak of Hopegill Head and Sand Hill beyond, with Grisedale Pike peering through the gap; this is quite simply superb! I don't know what I would do without my camera to slow me down a bit.

As you gain the end of the ridge, don't be misled into thinking the nearby cairn marks the summit, it doesn't. The highest point lies a short distance further along the ridge, by-passed by the path, but marked by a small cairn on the very edge of the drop to Gasgale Gill, a view in many ways mirroring that of Glenderaterra Beck from the east summit of Lonscale Fell.

DISTANCE: 2.2 kilometres (1.4 miles)
ASCENT: 570 metres (1870 feet)

The continuation to Hopegill Head offers no choice of route. Follow the superb ridge to a dramatic final rise to the summit.

DISTANCE: 1 kilometre (0.6 miles)
ASCENT: 95 metres (310 feet)

The link between Hopegill Head and Ladyside Pike is described in Route 2.5. The descent to Coledale Hause, starting off south east then south, crosses the minor top, Sand Hill first, on a broad, grassy path.

To continue to Grisedale Pike and its attendant un-named second summit, follow the edge of Hobcarton Crag, taking care in winter when this becomes heavily

corniced, to the depression between the two mountains, and then ascend to the unnamed summit and Grisedale Pike along the line of a collapsed wall. The retrospective view of Hobcarton Crag is impressive, though the crags are too friable to offer much sport to rock-climbers.
DISTANCE: 1.6 kilometres (1 mile)
ASCENT: 155 metres (510 feet)

Route 2.7 Grasmoor from Lanthwaite Green via Gasgale Gill For such an imposing and inviting mountain Grasmoor offers few natural lines of ascent. The steep face it presents to Crummock Water, Grasmoor End, is broken and scarred, and routes up it are more wishful thinking than anything else. You can get through, but my advice is to forget it, you will spend far too much time preoccupied with survival to enjoy what you are doing! The long ascent from Braithwaite (Route 2.9) is the easiest, and the way up Lad Hows from Rannerdale (Route 2.8) the shortest, but the route through the narrow defile of Gasgale Gill, though circuitous, has much to commend it.

Leave the car park at 158207 and follow the broad green path to the wooden bridge mentioned in Route 2.6. Here, turn right on to a clear path using which, with a few ups and downs, mostly created by landslips, you can court the splendid cascades and pools of the gill all the way to Coledale Hause. The path out of the gill doesn't in fact place you on the hause proper, but a short way above it. For the ascent of Grasmoor this is of no consequence for Gasgale Gill changes direction here, heading south to another col, between Crag Hill, to the east, and Grasmoor itself. Follow the good path on the east bank of the gill until you reach the upper col, and there turn right to take the path leading to the vast summit plateau of Grasmoor. The highest point is marked by a large cairn-cum-shelter.
DISTANCE: 5 kilometres (3.1 miles)
ASCENT: 700 metres (2295 feet)

Route 2.8 Grasmoor from Rannerdale via Lad Hows

Viewed from Cinderdale Common, where Cinderdale Beck flows down to Crummock Water, Lad Hows appears as a quite distinct fell, with no apparent link to the much higher mountain to the north. The connection, when finally it is discovered, lies further back, a long curving ridge flanked by Cinderdale Beck and Grasmoor on the one hand, and Rannerdale Beck and the long, narrow ridge of Whiteless Edge on the other. As a line of ascent Lad Hows demands constant energy, never easing much, but provides an entertaining and attractive way to the summit.

Leave the road by the car park at the foot of Cinderdale Common (164196) and follow the course of Cinderdale Beck for a short distance until you can comfortably cross it. Then continue on a narrow path not far from the true left bank of the beck, later climbing away from it to head for a small cairn marking the top of Lad Hows. Only here does the true form of the ridge come into perspective, curving and rising more steeply now to join the summit plateau near a moderate cairn, beyond which the highest point is identified by a multi-directional three star shelter-cairn.

DISTANCE: 2.6 kilometres (1.6 miles)
ASCENT: 735 metres (2410 feet)

The continuation to Crag Hill lies due east, pursuing a line of cairns until a prominent path comes into view and leads you unerringly to the col, normally identified (except in the driest conditions) by two tiny tarns, between the two mountains. The route up Crag Hill lies directly ahead, leading initially to the rim above Addacombe Hole (not named on the 1:50000 map), from where an easy ascent, left, will take you to the summit.

DISTANCE: 1.9 kilometres (1.2 miles)
ASCENT: 115 metres (380 feet)

Storm clouds threaten snow-capped Grasmoor. ▶

To continue instead to Wandope (an excellent proposal if you then intend to continue over Whiteless Pike either to Buttermere, or to return to Cinderdale Common through Rannerdale), leave the col between Grasmoor and Crag Hill by a narrow track heading south east, directly for Wandope. This is easy walking, on springy moss turf. The path eventually disappears, but by keeping to ascending ground you will come finally to the precipice at the edge of which stands the small cairn marking Wandope's highest point.

DISTANCE: 1.5 kilometres (0.9 miles)
ASCENT: 50 metres (165 feet)

If you intend to return from Grasmoor back down Lad Hows, the start of the descent is not clear. Leave the summit shelter and return to the moderate cairn a short distance east. At this point you pick up the prominent track leading to Crag Hill col, but don't follow it too far. Look for a small cairn just to the right of the track in a dip, and here head south east until you regain the path by which you ascended. If you are intent on returning this way in misty conditions, it will pay you to study the lie of the land for a minute or so on the way up before pressing on to the summit.

Route 2.9 Grasmoor from Braithwaite via Coledale Hause Like so many places in the Lake District, the head of Coledale lies scarred by evidence of man's need to gain minerals and wealth from the mountains, in this case cobalt. Screes of spoil and unsightly buildings, from time to time still in use, mar what once must have been an attractive landscape, and not even the towering mass of Force Crag, from which the mine takes its name, can divert attention for long from the pitiable mess beneath it. Thankfully, the mine is tucked away in the top corner of the valley, and, unlike the Coniston and Carrock mines, the walker need not approach it on the way to the fells.

It seems hypocritical then to ask you to make use of the old mine road to reach Coledale Hause, but the fact remains that it is a simple and direct way through. Start as for Route 2.3 from the small parking area a short way out of Braithwaite on the Whinlatter road. From one side of the area a stepped path ascends steeply (this is Route 2.3), while from the opposite side the mine road, much broader, starts its long and easy journey into Coledale. Follow this, rising gently above Coledale Beck below (watch for dippers and sandpipers here), and then running parallel with it all the way to the mine.

As you approach the mine, descend left to cross the beck, using boulders in the stream, and follow the conspicuous broad track curving round the head of the valley to what appears to be the hause. What you will find

The Grasmoor group and Mellbreak from the slopes of Great Borne.

however is not the hause you expect but another impressive cirque of mountains, this two-tiered cirque giving Coledale a unique feature that is worth a visit in itself. The paths shown on Ordnance Survey maps suggest that you can reach this upper cirque simply by continuing past the mine buildings and ascending on the left of Force Crag. So you may, but I would strongly counsel against it, especially in view of its unstable nature and with such an easy alternative close by.

In the upper cirque continue with the path, which is cairned and leads you not as you might think on to Coledale Hause but directly into the long, shallow valley between Crag Hill (on the left) and Grasmoor. This is fine, because this is where you want to be, but if you want to use the hause, look for a line of three or four cairns heading right from the path a short way below the hause. The line soon ends, but an extension of it places you squarely in the middle of the hause and facing the descent into Gasgale Gill, heading for Lanthwaite Green.

To continue to Grasmoor simply stay on the main path out of Coledale, swinging left to follow the line of upper Gasgale Gill, here flowing roughly south to north, until you reach a broad area of more or less level ground at the col between Crag Hill and Grasmoor. Here turn right and follow a path climbing easily to the summit plateau of Grasmoor. A large cairn-cum-shelter marks the highest point.

DISTANCE: 6.8 kilometres (4.25 miles)
ASCENT: 750 metres (2460 feet)

By returning to the col you can ascend north of east to the summit of Crag Hill, from where a reversal of Route 2.4 will take you to Stonycroft. The last paragraph of Route 2.4 describes a pleasant link between Stonycroft and Braithwaite should you need to return to the start.

Route 2.10 Whiteless Pike and Wandope The direct ascent of Whiteless Pike from Buttermere is a popular

The Grasmoor range from the summit of Haystacks.

and easy undertaking, but the alternative way, through Rannerdale, though enclosed, is remarkably beautiful.

2.10a From Buttermere Start near the quarry at 173172 and walk a short distance towards Buttermere until you can ascend to a gate at the end of a wall. Beyond the gate, follow the clear path which can be seen rising across the grassy fellside ahead. Alternatively, stay on the road a few strides further to gain a broad path behind Crag Houses which leads eventually into Newlands. Follow this path through a gate, and shortly after you reach a wall, leave it, left, to ascend through grass and bracken, to join the start mentioned above. The route climbs uneventfully to a col, with Rannerdale on your left, beyond which the path zig-zags a little before scampering

delightfully up Whiteless Breast to a final pull to Whiteless Pike itself; the summit is marked by a small cairn.
DISTANCE: 2.2 kilometres (1.4 miles)
ASCENT: 520 metres (1705 feet)

2.10b By Rannerdale North of the village of Buttermere the ground rises sharply into an elongated, knuckled ridge, the culminating point of which is called Rannerdale Knotts. Many centuries ago, before the rock of Hause Point, which then fell sheer into the water, was blasted away, this formidable ridge was an effective barrier, protecting the people of Buttermere from the invading Normans. Beyond lies the narrow and beautiful valley of Rannerdale itself, entered either from directly beneath the towering crags of Rannerdale Knotts, or, further north, from Cinderdale Common. Travelling in to Rannerdale from the wide open spaces of Cinderdale in the spring you will encounter the most unbelievable expanse of intensely-coloured bluebells. Couple this with the splendid tale of how the men and women of Buttermere repelled the Normans at the end of the eleventh century, vividly and romantically related in Nicholas Size's *The Secret Valley*, which, among other things tells how "It was hopeless to try and bury the great piles of Norman dead", and how Rannerdale valley "was like a charnel house", and you will, perhaps, find something veracious about Omar Khayyam's notion that "the loveliest flowers may spring from some dead Caesar's breast".

From Cinderdale Common follow Cinderdale Beck for only a short distance until you can cross it on a broad track. Follow this track towards Rannerdale valley where, just after you cross a stile, you will encounter the bluebell fields. Continue a little further to a sign directing you to a bridge across Rannerdale Beck and to a stile over the intake wall.

This same spot is reached from the small car park immediately beneath Rannerdale Knotts by following the obvious path, which leads eventually to the stile.

Cross the stile and follow a good path climbing easily through the valley until, finally, you arrive at the col between Whiteless Breast and the eastern end of Rannerdale Knotts. Here you join Route 2.10a for the final journey to the summit.

DISTANCE: 3.5 kilometres (2.2 miles)
ASCENT: 545 metres (1790 feet)

The continuation to Wandope traverses a fine, narrow ridge, rising first to a cairn, Thirdgill Head Man (not named on maps), on the extreme south western edge of Wandope. From here a path continues northwards to Coledale Hause, and in poor visibility it is easy to mistake the cairn and the ensuing path for the true summit of Wandope, which lies five hundred metres north of west across trackless, moss turf.

DISTANCE: 1.3 kilometres (0.8 miles)
ASCENT: 150 metres (490 feet)

If you chance to be travelling in the opposite direction, that is from Wandope to Whiteless Pike – which preceded by Grasmoor makes an excellent day – take great care in misty conditions to start off west from Wandope; there is a considerable risk of being inadvertently lulled into following Wandope's south ridge in the belief that it leads to Whiteless Pike – it doesn't, it leads only down to Third Gill (not named on the 1:50000 map) and Sail Beck, the retreat from which, by the time you discover your error, is quite daunting.

Route 2.11 Outside Sandwiched between much grander fare, with the Causey Pike ridge to the south and, across the deep recess of Coledale, Grisedale Pike to the north, Outside tends to be neglected. Positioned elsewhere it would however be a popular summit, in spite of its lack of height – purely in terms, that is, of what some folk think as necessary before a mountain is a mountain! Had I known how to interpret all those brown

Whiteless Pike and Rannerdale Knotts seen across Crummock Water.

lines on maps when I tackled Causey Pike on my first ever trip to Lakeland, I would undoubtedly have returned from Sail Gap over Outerside instead of plodding down the old mine road to Stair; map reading is confusing to a novice, and I obviously felt convinced Outerside was way out of my way. Silly man!

2.11a From Stonycroft Outerside presents a steep face to Coledale which belies the far less formidable approach from Stonycroft.

Start along the old mine road which accompanies Stonycroft Gill (not named on the 1:50000 map), and ascend uneventfully to the area of level ground south west of Outerside, known as High Moss. From here the rocky summit may be reached by an easy ascent of the fellside, north east.

DISTANCE: 2.8 kilometres (1.75 miles)
ASCENT: 430 metres (1410 feet)

2.11b From Braithwaite The ascent from Braithwaite seems sadly neglected, but it is one of Lakeland's more pleasurable short walks. The initial objective is High Coledale farm (226228), beyond which the open fellside is gained. Immediately ahead rises the lump of Stile End, approached by a grassy path, which later divides into three, all routes then passing through stretches of bracken. The path to the left leads to Barrow Door, and affords an easy scamper up Barrow; the central path tackles Stile End head on, while the third rises to the right, making for the col, Low Moss, between Stile End and Outerside. From Low Moss (not named on the 1:50000 map) on which there is a tiny tarn, cross a section of heather ascending the slopes of Outerside to a final grassy stretch to the summit.
DISTANCE: 3 kilometres (1.9 miles)
ASCENT: 470 metres (1540 feet)

Route 2.12 Ard Crags and Knott Rigg The ridge of Knott Rigg and Ard Crags is linked tenuously, at Newlands Hause, to the much higher Robinson and its neighbours, Hindscarth and Dalehead, though you wouldn't think so. But careful study of the map reveals that it is sandwiched between Sail Beck, on the west, flowing south west, and parallel Keskadale Beck, on the east, flowing in quite the opposite direction; only the road across the hause isolates it from its true place in the scheme of things. Given a perfect summer's day, Knott Rigg, nearer the hause than Ard Crags, can be sauntered up by folk of any age; children skip up it, grandmothers take it a little more easily, but get there all the same, hill-walkers in the main find it too demeaning. Yet it has the distinction of being the only summit in Lakeland that I have had to reach on all fours, clinging tenaciously to every blade of gnarled rock and wiry tuft of heather, as a furious Force 11 wind whipped its narrow crest.

From the car parks on either side of Newlands Hause it is a simple walk to Knott Rigg over springy turf, and requires no detailed description. From the hause a path rising to the summit of the ridge is plainly in view, and you should use this to gain the ridge, whereupon there is an impressive view down into Sail Beck, and across to Wandope, Sail and Crag Hill.

DISTANCE: 1.3 kilometres (0.8 miles)
ASCENT: 225 metres (740 feet)

From Keskadale (211193), where Ill Gill (not named on the 1:50000 map) appears from behind the north east ridge of Knott Rigg, the stream can be crossed to gain a path climbing steeply at first up a series of minor bumps to the summit. There is easier ground lower down the hillside, on the left, but the ridge route is a splendid little challenge.

DISTANCE: 1.4 kilometres (0.9 miles)
ASCENT: 315 metres (1035 feet)

Knott Rigg is simply the southernmost extremity of a short ridge, the northern end of which gathers together to form shapely Ard Crags, a slightly higher summit. An approach from the north should start where Rigg Beck flows beneath the valley road (230201). Near some old quarry workings take the path alongside Rigg Beck, which incidentally is a splendid little traverse of the hills, running behind Ard Crags and Knott Rigg to Buttermere. Follow the path until a wall descends on the left, then cross the stream to gain the steep bracken-clad fellside above. The route is clear enough, tackling first the rocky outcrop, Aikin Knott, before ascending to an east summit, beyond which lies the highest point.

DISTANCE: 2.4 kilometres (1.5 miles)
ASCENT: 415 metres (1360 feet)

The whole ridge is excellent for off-days and easy days, and well worth a visit.

Section 3 – The Newlands Fells

	MAP REFERENCE	HEIGHT (m)	OS 1:50000 MAP
Dale Head	223153	753	89/90
Robinson	202169	737	89/90
Hindscarth	215165	727	89/90
High Spy	234162	653	89/90
Maiden Moor	237182	576	89/90
Cat Bells	244198	451	89/90

ROUTES

3.1   Dale Head from Honister
3.2   Hindscarth from Newlands
3.3   Robinson from Buttermere
3.4   Robinson from Newlands
3.5   High Spy from Seatoller
3.6   Maiden Moor and High Spy from Manesty
3.7   Cat Bells from Manesty

The Newlands Fells are one of the smallest groups of hills in the Lake District, lying south west of Derwentwater, the northern end of which, at Keswick, is linked by the beautiful Newlands valley to Buttermere. The group in spite of its modest compass boasts two splendid ridges, roughly at right angles, and a fine selection of shapely and attractive summits. Though it is not readily apparent, the whole group, together with those superb fells of Grasmoor, Grisedale and Whinlatter to the north, are contained within the catchment area of one river, the Derwent, for the River Cocker, which flows west from the top of Honister Pass and through Buttermere and Crummock Water, is but a tributary of the Derwent, the two joining forces, predictably, at Cockermouth.

The underlying rocks of this inviting region are Skiddaw Slates, formed as muds in an ancient sea and later hardened and cleaved into slates. They betray themselves in the characteristic smooth shapes of the fells, the general absence of tarns, and a vegetation mainly of grass and heather.

Like many other places in the Lake District the New-lands Fells have seen their share of mining activity. At the Goldscope Mine in the Newlands valley, beneath the towering slopes of High Spy and Dale Head, copper was mined as early as the thirteenth century from a vein nine feet thick and exceptionally rich in workable copper. The mine also produced large amounts of lead, a small amount of silver and, so it is said, a modicum of gold. Not unexpectedly Goldscope, a name first appearing in records in 1569 as *Gottesgab* or God's Gift, was one of Lakeland's most prosperous mines. Its greatest period of production, in a history spanning several centuries, was in the six-teenth century during the reign of Elizabeth I. Concerned that the country should be less dependent on foreign supplies, Elizabeth and her chief minister, Lord Burghley, made a serious attempt to exploit our own resources. German miners were brought across, and pro-duction encouraged by the granting of royal patronage with the setting up, in 1561, of The Society for the Mines Royal, and by the award of hidden subsidies in the form of waived taxes. The Society also worked Dale Head Mine, high up on the fellside, and there were other mines elsewhere in the Newlands valley. Ore was taken by packhorse to the shores of Derwentwater, at a place which became known as Copperhead Hill (253216), and from there to the smelter on the banks of the River Greta at Brigham, on the outskirts of Keswick. Having passed through Brigham the copper then had to receive the Queen's mark, given at the Receiving House, now the Moot Hall, in Keswick.

Thankfully the mines of the Newlands Fells are well off the beaten track, and do not intrude quite so blatantly as elsewhere. The result is an area of abundant tranquil-lity, pastoral reflection, and high, soaring ridges pressing steeply on the valleys from which they rise like leviathans crammed into a small space.

Cat Bells is an easy and popular ascent, as is this continuation to Maiden Moor and High Spy.

Route 3.1 Dale Head from Honister The magnificent summit cairn on Dale Head overlooks the valley or dale of Newlands, which prompted its name. It is a valley wealthy in minerals, and enclosed dramatically on the east by the fine Maiden Moor–High Spy ridge, and on the west by the northern spur of the adjacent fell, Hindscarth. These smooth-sided fells are the product of the underlying Skiddaw Slate, but it is on Dale Head, and along the ridge running west to Robinson that the geological interface occurs between the ancient slate and the much younger igneous rocks of the Borrowdale Volcanic Series.

At the end of the last century, Herman Prior, author of the *Pedestrian and General Guide to the Lake District of England* (which incidentally contains some magnificent pedestrian itineraries of up to twenty-one days' duration), recommended the ascent from the top of the Honister Pass "because advantage may be taken of the Buttermere

Along the High Spy ridge.

Dale Head from High Spy.

wagonettes any morning". There are few wagonettes in evidence these days, but the way up from Honister, unless you have walked there from Seatoller, is unlikely to cause any problems.

Leave the car park behind the youth hostel (225136), at the top of the pass, cross the road, and ascend on the right of the fence-line. The fence disappears half way up the fellside, but there is a good path all the way which leads you unerringly to the top.

DISTANCE: 1.8 kilometres (1.1 miles)
ASCENT: 395 metres (1295 feet)

The continuation along the ridge to Hindscarth, along predictably-named Hindscarth Edge (though not on the 1:50 000 map), is delineated on your right by the steep drop to the Newlands valley and on your left by the even steeper fall to the upper reaches of the Buttermere valley.

Go west from Dale Head summit on a clear path which

Dale Head from Grey Knotts.

descends to a narrowing in the ridge before a short rocky ascent. There are the remains of a fence along the top of the ridge, which serves as an adequate guide, and leads to the start of a line of cairns heading right, at the top of a small rise and away from the main ridge, to the summit of Hindscarth.

DISTANCE: 1.7 kilometres (1 mile)
ASCENT: 75 metres (245 feet)

For High Spy, leave Dale Head going east, taking care not to follow the curving north east ridge which leads to the precipitous Dale Head crags and trouble. The route to the col and Dalehead Tarn is cairned and aims for the south side of the tarn, before ascending east of north on a rough path to the summit cairn.

DISTANCE: 1.9 kilometres (1.2 miles)
ASCENT: 155 metres (505 feet)

Dale Head and the upper Newlands valley.

An excellent path leads from Scope End in the Newlands valley to Hindscarth.

Route 3.2 Hindscarth from Newlands Newlands valley must be one of the most idyllic in Lakeland; farms sit prettily in the middle of neatly-patterned fields dotted with sheep and bordered with willow, ash, sycamore and oak. Red squirrels share the tree tops with jays, thrushes, cuckoos, pipits, and a variety of tits – great, blue, long-tailed, coal and willow – while skylarks, buzzards, ravens and kestrels can be spotted overhead. Hindscarth itself, the 'pass of the deer', is without question the shapeliest of fells, its great tilted peak and attendant ridge starkly etched against the sky. And, as befits this fine fell, the ascent from Newlands, along the ridge of Scope End, is excellent, and quite unsuspected if you view the mountain from Buttermere.

The key to the ascent of Scope End is Newlands Chapel (230194); distance and ascent are measured from there, but there is nowhere to park, and I find it easier to park at Rigg Beck (229202) where a disused quarry has been turned to good advantage. (Add 1 kilometre (0.6 miles).)

Take the track on the left, just past the chapel, and follow this to Low Snab farm. Pass through a gate to gain the open fellside, though the most immediate sight to draw one's attention are the waste spills of the Goldscope Mine, which also operated on the opposite side of the valley. I don't recommend you to venture into the workings, you would need a torch, and they *are* dangerous.

Follow the wall behind Low Snab farm for a short distance, and then ascend left to gain Scope End. The going is steep at first, but there is a clear path, and when the initial pull is completed, and with the whole ridge to Hindscarth stretching before you, the splendour of the situation easily overcomes any weariness. Continue, lazily I recommend, along the ridge, narrow in places, with a path that cavorts up and down, switching from one side of the ridge to the other, inviting you to enjoy yourself. Not even the final pull to the summit can spoil what has gone before, unless you are disappointed to find that the prominent 'cairn' – a circular shelter, in fact – which has been in view all the way is a false summit; the true summit, marked by a modest cairn in the middle of a large stony plateau, lies a short way further on.

DISTANCE: 3.3 kilometres (2 miles)
ASCENT: 590 metres (1935 feet)

A cairned path leads south from the summit to a small prominence on which appears the occasional remnant of an old fence-line and a clear pathway. This path may be followed, left, to Dalehead, placing you precisely at the summit.

DISTANCE: 1.6 kilometres (1 mile)
ASCENT: 100 metres (330 feet)

Or you can go right, to Robinson, en route to which you will encounter a new fence-line climbing to a large cairn on reaching which you must head north across stony ground to the highest point, another large cairn on a low rocky outcrop.

DISTANCE: 2.3 kilometres (1.4 miles)
ASCENT: 160 metres (525 feet)

Route 3.3 Robinson from Buttermere Robinson is another mountain, like its neighbour Hindscarth, which offers its riches to the north, dominating the village of Buttermere, as a rounded, unappealing dome. But its ascent from the village is popular, and affords splendid views across Buttermere of the massive High Stile range, and of Grasmoor and its satellites. The fell was named after one Richard Robinson, a local worthy, who, quick to perceive the opportunities afforded by the Dissolution of the Monasteries (the Monks owned a good chunk of Lakeland), purchased it during the reign of Henry VIII.

Leave Buttermere by starting up the road ascending north east from Buttermere across Newlands Hause. At a small lay-by on the right (179171) take the obvious grassy path (an old road used for bringing peat down) until you crest the first major objective, High Snockrigg. Beyond you stretches Buttermere Moss, a marshy expanse that cannot be avoided, though slightly better ground can be found by keeping to the right. It is only here that Robinson comes into view.

Cross the Moss to regain dry ground, and follow the cairned, rising track which leads to a large cairn on the edge of the summit plateau. The main summit cairn lies a short distance away on a low rocky outcrop.

DISTANCE: 2.8 kilometres (1.75 miles)
ASCENT: 625 metres (2050 feet)

To continue to Hindscarth head south from the summit, descending only slightly at first, until you encounter a large cairn near a new fence-line. Go left here, descending more steeply now on a good path, to the col between the two mountains, at the head of Little Dale, and ascend

steeply by Littledale Edge, to the southern edge of Hindscarth's summit plateau where a left turn, north, will take
you easily to the summit. Note that the new fence-line
ends at the col.

DISTANCE: 2.3 kilometres (1.4 miles)
ASCENT: 150 metres (490 feet)

Route 3.4 Robinson from Newlands Everything said
in Route 3.2 about the delights of Newlands valley as
experienced on the ascent of Hindscarth applies equally
here, of course. Both mountains also have long north
ridges with the wide, grassy expanse of Little Dale between them, though Robinson has rather more mountain
and a little less ridge than Hindscarth.

3.4a From Newlands valley Again, the key is Newlands
Chapel (230194), but observe my remarks about parking.
At the chapel, instead of going left, as you would for
Scope End, continue ahead on a road to Low High Snab
farm (222189 – not named on the 1:50000 map, nor is it
a contradiction in terms!) from where a Permissive Path
takes you between walled and fenced enclosures on to the
open fellside. Once clear of the farm ascend steeply, right,
on a clear path to gain the northern end of High Snab
Bank, and then follow a splendidly airy grassy path
towards the distant mound of Robinson.

As you approach Robinson, leaving the grassy ridge
behind, there are two significant rock steps and a small
one, all requiring hands as well as feet, and calling for a
fair bit of squirming about if you are descending by this
route with a sizeable pack on.

Above the rock steps a line of cairns leads you first to
the one prominent cairn you will have seen from below,
and no doubt hoped was the summit. On reaching it you
will find your hopes dashed, the main summit lies a short
distance further on.

DISTANCE: 4 kilometres (2.5 miles)
ASCENT: 595 metres (1950 feet)

If you are descending by this route in poor visibility take care not to be led astray by cairns which simply lead to vantage points overlooking Little Dale, especially on the summit plateau.

3.4b From Newlands Hause Probably because it is the shortest ascent of Robinson this route seems to have a certain popularity, but it is pretty boring!

From Newlands Hause ascend the clear track rising steeply through broken ground some distance to the right of the waterfalls – don't make for the falls themselves. As the gradient eases Buttermere Moss comes into view and presents you with two alternatives. You can attempt to make a rough bee-line for Robinson, but, although vague tracks do appear, it is better only to contemplate this after prolonged dry weather. Or, wiser, you can continue towards High Snockrigg and there join Route 3.3, circum-navigating Buttermere Moss on the south side.

DISTANCE: 2.2 kilometres (1.4 miles)
ASCENT: 405 metres (1330 feet)

The north-east ridge of Robinson from the Scope End route to Hindscarth.

Route 3.5 High Spy from Seatoller The various ascents to High Spy (and for that matter, Dale Head) from the southern end of Borrowdale, from Rosthwaite to Seatoller, are all a bit scrappy and grim, being better reserved as means of descent. But a way can be worked out from Seatoller which has some merit, and is suitable for a short day.

At 235138, part way up the Honister Pass, a bridleway (sign-posted) leaves the roadway heading east. After about 1 kilometre (0.6 miles) this track curves northwards and later passes the foot of Tongue Gill (not named on the 1:50 000 map). By driving up the pass and starting along this bridleway you save some ascent, but the track may be joined without too much effort from Seatoller itself.

Leave the car park at Seatoller and join the road over Honister, but just after the last buildings take a gate on the right, to gain a broad track. This track soon doubles back, left, and climbs to the intake wall. Before reaching the wall, where there is a gate, you can short-cut right, to another, narrow gate, at which point (242142) you join the bridleway.

A short way further on, near a stile over the wall on your right, you cross Scaleforce Gill by a new wooden bridge with a gate at each end. This section of bridleway is part of one of Lakeland's longer distance walks, the Allerdale Ramble, and between Seatoller and Grange provides what must surely be the finest low-level walk in Lakeland, passing as it does, by the famous volcanic wedge in the Jaws of Borrowdale, Castle Crag (250160), an imposing, tree-girt, steep-sided pedestal, easily gained from the track, and an excellent vantage point.

About 250 metres beyond the bridge, take a narrow path ascending left, and obviously making for the deep gash of Tongue Gill (245152). Eventually you will arrive at a group of derelict quarry buildings, one of which has been converted into a climbing hut. The quarries, Rigghead, produced slate from levels well inside the hillside, and many of the adits may still be entered and provide excellent shelter in bad weather, but they are dangerous and should not be explored too far.

Continue beyond the quarries by an indistinct path linking the foot of each of the nearby spoil heaps until you can join a better path ascending along Tongue Gill from Borrowdale. At the highest level, close by a large open adit on your left, a small platform is reached on which two cairns indicate the way to the final section of pathway out of the gill. This path now culminates in a new fence-line, crossed by a step stile, and beyond which is a large cairn. In misty conditions this area is confusing. Not far from the large cairn are two smaller ones. If you aim for the one on the left, you end up paralleling the fence-line, and climb southwards, eventually to arrive at Launchy Tarn, shown but not named on the 1:50000 at 234149. For High Spy you should aim for the second cairn on the right and perched on a low outcrop of rock. This gives the direction of yet another cairn, about eighty metres distant across a stretch of marshy ground. But by heading in that direction (roughly north west) you will intersect a rough, cairned path ascending from Dalehead Tarn, which you can then follow to the summit plateau, a broad expanse with many minor rock outcrops.

DISTANCE: 4 kilometres (2.5 miles)
ASCENT: 535 metres (1755 feet)

Route 3.6 Maiden Moor and High Spy from Manesty

Motorists travelling down Borrowdale cannot fail to be impressed by the soaring heights behind the village of Grange. Sporting a variety of names – Nitting Haws, Lobstone Band, Goat Crag and Low Scawdell – they present a rugged countenance to the valley and must be one of the most lasting impressions every visitor to Lakeland takes away with them. These rough and scarred faces rise to culminate in a fine ridge extending from Swinside in the north to overlook Seatoller in the south before taking a dog-leg to continue in splendid fashion to Buttermere. The complete traverse, Swinside to

Newlands Hause and Robinson seen from the Scale Force path above Buttermere.

Buttermere, is highly recommended. The section between Maiden Moor and High Spy however is usually sufficient for a shortish day, especially if Cat Bells is included (Route 3.7). The usual start is from Manesty (251185) on the western side of the valley.

Just north of the village take a broad ascending path on the left, which has seen improvement work in recent years, and follow this without difficulty – though the occasional time-out to admire the scenery, especially across Derwent Water, is more than justified. The top of the path ends in a series of fenced runnels, intended to guide walkers away from the more eroded pathways, so that they can create new eroded pathways of their own – and then, presumably, revert back to the old ones! This is Hause Gate (not named as such on the 1:50 000 map), a grassy col between Cat Bells on the one hand and Maiden Moor on the other.

Continue left and upwards on a broad path, which,

by-passing Maiden Moor en route (though it can be taken in easily), now proceeds all the way to the large summit cairn on High Spy without incident.

DISTANCE: 4.3 kilometres (2.7 miles)
ASCENT: 555 metres (1820 feet)

This is excellent, airy walking; on your left the ground falls to Borrowdale, while to the right it plummets in rugged style to the wild and secluded upper reaches of the Newlands valley where most of the mining activity took place. The whole of the western flank of High Spy is taken up with an impressive array of cliffs, Eel Crags, their appearance rather broken, but nevertheless sustaining a few high-graded rock-climbing routes.

Route 3.5 describes an ascent from the vicinity of Seatoller, which serves just as well as a descent for walkers who do not need to return to Manesty.

Route 3.7 Cat Bells from Manesty This is a simple stroll, with a splendid reward in the fine prospect it opens up of Derwent Water, Keswick and the Skiddaw fells.

From Manesty (251185) follow the path mentioned in Route 3.6 to Hause Gate and there turn right, north, to follow a gently ascending path to the neat rocky crown of Cat Bells.

DISTANCE: 1.7 kilometres (1 mile)
ASCENT: 355 metres (1165 feet)

A concluding descent northwards, over Brandlehow, to Gutherscale or Swinside, followed by a return along the roadway to Manesty, is an excellent way of filling a short day. Such a route can, of course, be reversed, with equal pleasure.

Prominent in the view of Derwent Water from this short ridge is St. Herbert's Island, which among the beautiful isles of Derwent Water deserves more than a passing mention. St. Herbert, who was a friend of the better known St. Cuthbert, according to the Venerable

Bede chose the island for his hermitage "to avoid the intercourse of man, and that nothing might withdraw his attention from unceasing mortification and prayer". Each year Herbert met Cuthbert in Carlisle, but in 687 Cuthbert, having a presentiment of his death, told Herbert that he would not see him again. "When Herberte heard this, he fell down at his feet, and with many sighs and tears beseeched him, for the love of the Lord, that he would not forsake him, but to remember his faithful brother and associate, and make intercession with the gracious God, that they might depart hence into heaven together." The request was granted, and both men died on the 19th day of March, 687, at the same hour.

Wordsworth also records the story in 'The Hermit of Derwent Water':

> . . . stranger, not unmoved
> Wilt thou behold this shapeless heap of stones,
> The desolate ruins of St. Herbert's cell.
> There stood his threshold; there was spread the roof
> That sheltered him, a self-secluded man.

Section 4 – The High Stile Range

	MAP REFERENCE	HEIGHT (m)	OS 1:50 000 MAP
High Stile	170148	807	89
Red Pike	160155	755	89
High Crag	181140	744	89/90
Dodd	164158	641	89
Starling Dodd	142158	633	89
Great Borne (Herdus)	124164	616	89
Hay Stacks	193131	597	89/90
Blake Fell	110197	573	89
Gavel Fell	117185	526	89
Mellbreak	149186	512	89
Hen Comb	132181	509	89

ROUTES
4.1 The Loweswater Fells
4.2 Scale Force, Floutern Tarn and Great Borne from Buttermere
4.3 Red Pike and Starling Dodd from Buttermere
4.4 Red Pike, High Stile and High Crag from Buttermere
4.5 Scarth Gap and High Crag
4.6 Hay Stacks
4.7 Great Borne from Ennerdale

"Buttermere and Crummock," wrote W.G. Collingwood, "are Nature's art for art's sake." To stand on the sediment-covered rock sill separating what was once a single lake is to experience this art in good measure; to the south the massive wall of the High Stile range, a complex geological interface of pink granophyre and Skiddaw slates, bars easy access to the neighbouring valley of Ennerdale. North and east rise the Grasmoor group of fells and the Buttermere Fells, Robinson, Hindscarth and distant Dalehead, the latter closing in the upper end of the valley, in concert with the rugged profile of Honister Crag and Fleetwith Pike, a scene which in the nineteenth century moved Turner to paint his well-known study of primeval light and darkness, now in the Tate Gallery. But to gain the fullest appreciation you must languish along the western approaches, coming from Cockermouth, or over Whinlatter from Keswick, soaking up the pasturelands of the Vale of Lorton; sparing a moment for Lanthwaite, site of an ancient British settlement, and the side valley of Loweswater before quietly enjoying your first glimpse of Crummock Water. Take your time as you pass beneath Grasmoor and Rannerdale Knotts, with first Mellbreak, then the cone of Red Pike and the whole High Stile ridge, opening before you to the right until, at last, you see ahead the dark shape of Honister Crag and the wild valley head of Gatescarth.

The mountains do the valley justice; the High Stile

ridge is a magnificent traverse, especially if undertaken from end to end, though it lends itself all-too-readily to dissection at the centrally-placed Red Pike. But nothing spoils if you have to come back on another day, and the steep ascent of Red Pike is something with which you could easily develop a love–hate relationship, the effort of getting there offset by the rewards gained.

In the north west, the twin-topped Mellbreak serves as sentinel to this remarkable valley, rising sharply from Crummock Water, and conceals a small group of fells only infrequently visited, but admirable on a warm summer's day or in winter when the higher fells have their heads in the clouds. By contrast, at the other end of the range, Hay Stacks, a rugged interloper amid so many high and mighty fells, is, if anything, the finest of them all! For nowhere in Lakeland is there so diverse a concoction of rocky tors, tranquil tarns, heather trails, gorges, gables and grandeur; truly a summit to be lingered upon and explored, and every approach with its own delectable charms. May I be forgiven for putting my prejudices so prominently on display.

Route 4.1 The Loweswater Fells When first I visited the range of grassy fells that bring the Vale of Lorton to an abrupt end on its south-western extremity, it was with a resounding note of chagrin that for the then fifteen years of wandering I had spent among the Lake Mountains I had neglected them. That, I must confess, was a grave mistake, and one I strongly counsel you not to make. As an introduction to the rest of this most idyllic of valleys, the Loweswater Fells are an *hors-d'œuvre par excellence*. While higher fare is readily on hand, these rounded fells are more than capable of commanding your attention for days on end. What follows here is not an account of all there is to see and do, but a selection, a mere titillation, sufficient, I hope, to captivate you and lead you on to explore further for yourself.

4.1a Mellbreak Like its neighbour, Hen Comb, Mellbreak stands alone, without linking ridges to other fells or even a convenient expanse of dry ground to make the crossing from one to the other just that little bit easier. Rising above Crummock Water, it turns the head of many a walker on the far shore intent on a day on Grasmoor or the Whiteside ridge.

It may be ascended from Buttermere by the trail which leads to Scale Force and Floutern Tarn (Route 4.2), leaving that track once the edge of Mosedale is reached to totter up grassy slopes to the southernmost, the highest, top. But this is not the way to get the best out of Mellbreak.

Start instead in Loweswater village; you can park a car or two near the telephone box (143211). Take the road leading to the church, and there turn left and then immediately right to gain a road passing Kirkgate Farm (not named on the 1:50 000 map) until finally you come to a gate at the foot of a fire break through a narrow section of forest, shown, curiously, on the 1:50 000 map, but not on the larger 1:25 000 map!

Ascend through the fire break and immediately gain a broad grassy path making for the obvious, and seemingly daunting, tongue of scree spilling from the northern crags of the fell. A direct assault on the vertical scree run can be avoided by a series of zig-zags on the left, which also ease some of the leg work. But higher up, as a notch appears in the rocks above, the best line is a direct one.

Climb through the notch to another zig-zagging path which finally leads to a neat platform, the first real opportunity for a breather. A halt here is in any case essential, for if you take a few steps to your left, around a mini-buttress, you will be rewarded by a truly breathtaking view of Crummock Water, Rannerdale, Buttermere and distant Fleetwith Pike at its head. Face the other way, and the whole of the Vale of Lorton is spread at your feet, with its delectable attendant, Fellbarrow, and, further west, the elegant form of Loweswater itself.

If you can bring yourself to continue upwards, the way is now perfectly obvious, and needs no description. The first summit encountered however, marked by a sizeable cairn, is not the highest. To reach this you must descend southwards, on a reasonable, but damp, path, across a broad col, to a final easy pull to a much less distinguished summit cairn.

DISTANCE: 3 kilometres (1.9 miles)
ASCENT: 460 metres (1510 feet)

The return to Loweswater may be accomplished by the simple expedient of a steep descent westwards, taking care to avoid a few minor rock outcrops, until you intersect the valley path near a lone holly tree. Or, return to the col and descend to the west from there, when you may hit a slightly higher path than that through the valley bottom, taking you back to the fire break. This easy alternative may also be used as a line of ascent.

4.1b Hen Comb Hen Comb is a fell of simple structure, rising as a long grassy ridge to a finely-shaped peak. It is an uncomplicated affair, presenting no difficulties, save the hazard in wet weather of crossing Mosedale Beck.

Follow Route 4.1a to the foot of the firebreak, but then continue right for a short distance with the forest on one hand and a wall on the other, until the wall descends, right, to a gate at the junction with a fence. Pass through the gate and cross the beck – you may have to wade across if there has been much rain, or tackle Mellbreak instead. Once across ascend by a wall until a grassy path goes left, first to the minor bump, Little Dodd, and then to the summit, marked by a fine cairn.

DISTANCE: 3.5 kilometres (2.2 miles)
ASCENT: 390 metres (1280 feet)

4.1c Gavel Fell and Blake Fell These are the two highest of the Loweswater Fells, and may be conveniently combined in one walk from the National Trust car park at

Maggie's Bridge (135210 – not named on the 1:50000 map). If you like bilberries as well as walking, my advice is to leave Blake Fell to the end because its north-eastern extremity, Carling Knott, is so liberally endowed with them that in season you simply would go no further if you tackled that end first.

From the car park take the track leading to High Nook Farm and continue to a gate in the intake wall. Shortly after the intake, you have a choice. Either continue ahead, passing Highnook Tarn (not named on maps) to ascend by a zig-zag path up the tongue of fellside between the two branches of Highnook Beck; this route rises eventually to intersect a fence-line linking the two summits near the col between them. Or you can take an obvious path, left – an old drove road – leading towards Whiteoak Beck, leaving this as it starts to descend to the

In this picture the track from the Dubs Quarry to Haystacks (in shadow) is clearly seen. This makes an excellent variant to the Four Passes Walk.

Whiteoak valley for a narrow path, right, climbing around Black Crag, and then across virtually trackless ground to a cairn, not to be mistaken in mist for the summit. This is followed by a shallow, boggy depression before an easy pull to the top of Gavel Fell. A large cairn, on the far side of a fence, marks what is generally accepted as the summit, but fractionally higher ground can be found, unmarked, 150 metres north on the Loweswater side of the fence. As in other places, seeing is not believing.

DISTANCE: 3.3 kilometres (2 miles)
ASCENT: 400 metres (1310 feet)

The continuation to Blake Fell simply follows the fence-line through a series of dog-legs until, as you approach the summit, a couple of step stiles (more are needed, to give better access to and from Carling Knott) allow you to gain a path taking you to the circular shelter looking seaward that marks the highest point, a splendid airy elevation with a commanding view.

DISTANCE: 1.7 kilometres (1 mile)
ASCENT: 120 metres (395 feet)

Carling Knott is a long arm extending north east from Blake Fell. People with short legs will have difficulty crossing the new fence erected across the top of Blake Fell, and may have to retreat a few hundred metres to one of the step stiles. Once across the fence aim for a series of rocky ledges high above the head of Highnook valley, crossing one well-cairned top before descending to the top of Carling Knott. Ahead of you lies one of the steepest descents in Lakeland, with only a carpet of bilberries and the occasional sprig of heather to halt any slip. But the view from this point is utterly unbelievable; Loweswater and Holme Wood are so far below you they seem like some toyland landscape, while even rugged Grasmoor assumes a less aggressive demeanour.

An easier way down can be found however by going left, north west, from the summit, following the boundary

*The col of Scarth Gap separates High Crag, on the left, from Haystacks.
Black Sail Youth Hostel can just be picked out in the centre right.*

of the National Trust land, until you can swing back
right beneath Carling Knott on a path along the walled
boundary of Holme Wood. Follow this path to Highnook
Beck, crossed by a bridge, and then return to the gate in
the intake wall met with on the ascent, continuing to
Maggie's Bridge by the outward route.

If you are bounding with energy you can try ascending
by this route, but I don't commend it.

**Route 4.2 Scale Force, Floutern Tarn and Great Borne
from Buttermere** Only at each end does the High Stile
range offer any low level pedestrian way into the neighbouring Ennerdale, the route by Floutern Tarn being
by far the easiest, though possessing little of the rugged grandeur encountered on the entry by Scarth Gap,
below Hay Stacks. From Buttermere the way lies by the
Fish Hotel, along a well sign-posted track crossing the

alluvial link between Buttermere and Crummock Water.

At the turn of the eighteenth century the Fish was kept by a couple called Robinson who were blessed with a stunningly beautiful daughter, Mary, who used to wait at table. When only fourteen she was remarked on by Captain Budworth in his book, *A Fortnight's Ramble in the Lakes*, and became something of a local celebrity as the Beauty of Buttermere. When she was twenty-four Mary caught the eye of a personable visitor to the Fish. The Honourable Alexander Augustus Hope, Lieutenant-Colonel in the 14th Regiment of Foot, and brother to the Earl of Hopetoun, wooed and won the Beauty of Buttermere and they were married in Lorton church on 2nd October, 1802. Coleridge, a longstanding admirer of the local heroine, wrote a piece on the wedding for the *Morning Post* where it eventually came to the notice of the genuine Colonel Hope who had been abroad all the summer!

Inquiries followed which led to the detection of the imposture. Mary's Colonel Hope was, alas, one John Hatfield, who had only recently failed to obtain the hand of a young lady of fortune in Keswick but already had a second wife still living and children from two marriages. He was eventually hanged, not for bigamy, but forgery in Carlisle in September 1803. As for Mary, who bore him a child which died, her sorry tale became the stuff of melodrama on the London stage. She herself married again and lived into old age in the village of Caldbeck where she is buried, "but sorrow, like a cloud on the sun, shaded her soul".

Not far beyond the Fish Hotel a track (sign-posted) leads by Scale Bridge along the southern shore of Crummock Water, a most delightful passage, to Scale Force, the highest of all the Lakeland waterfalls, and the object of considerable nineteenth-century admiration. The gorge of Scale Force, still a popular low-level excursion (3 kilometres: 1.9 miles), is thought to be post-glacial, but the fall owes its present character to the contact of rocks of different degrees of hardness, debouching from the moorland above at a point where hard granophyre meets the easily-eroded, softer Skiddaw slates.

Follow the path beyond the Force, to climb steadily to the boggy expanse of Mosedale, with the bulk of Mellbreak on your right. Ahead, unseen, lies Floutern Tarn (flow-tarn, the tarn of the bog), and the ground between a broad, marshy tract of moorland, fed by numerous small streams. It is this unappetising *mélange* of adversity that discourages many walkers from visiting the area, but I feel the effort, particularly in summer, or when the ground is frozen, is well justified. The whole arena is an impressive sanctum, overlooked by the rugged heights of Great Borne, and among the quietest of Lakeland's quiet corners.

It isn't easy to find a totally dry way across the marsh, though a few stiles at fences suggest a way that leads eventually to a good path ascending to the north of Floutern Tarn. This takes you to the top of the pass, beyond which the path continues to the western end of Ennerdale Water.

At the top of the pass another fence is encountered, rocketing upwards very steeply, and without a break, to the summit plateau of Great Borne. More marshy ground at the pass necessitates a precarious passage, utilising stiles, before you can get to grips with the ascent. The summit of Great Borne is divided by the fence-line; the highest point, marked by a trig point, is on the south side, and offers a splendid panorama.

DISTANCE: 7 kilometres (4.4 miles)

ASCENT: 505 metres (1655 feet)

Route 4.3 Red Pike and Starling Dodd from Buttermere

The ascent of Red Pike from Buttermere is the key to two of the finest ridge walks in the Lake District, one, unquestionably the best, running south east over High Stile and High Crags to Hay Stacks, while the other, described here, has about it an enigmatic charm that gives it special appeal, particularly as an escape from

A wintry High Stile from Red Pike.

overcrowded routes elsewhere. Of course, they form two sections of the same ridge, and though the complete traverse is a splendid undertaking, it generally proves too much for most walkers. In any case, neither section is to be hastened over.

The route to Red Pike, starting down the track passing by the Fish Hotel, is well sign-posted and leads to the foot of Sour Milk Gill where it flows into Buttermere lake. Here the path enters Burtness Wood where much thinning of the mature larches has taken place in recent years, and replacement oak planted. Signs leave you in no doubt about the way, and it is only when you cross the lakeshore path and start to ascend steeply on a long diagonal through the trees that you pass the last of them. This long ascent, coming in the early part of the walk calls for considerable energy, but the speed with which you rise from the valley to gaze across to Robinson and Grasmoor makes the effort worthwhile.

The Chapel Crags of High Stile rise dramatically above Bleaberry Tarn.

Cross the upper boundary of Burtness Wood at a stile and ascend a reconstructed path, replacing one which used to be an abomination of loose, unstable stones. The going is still steep until you reach a grassy shelf (rather more peat and heather roots than grass) leading you back to the top of Sour Milk Gill. Here the path forks, one track going left to the concealed sanctuary of Bleaberry Tarn sheltering in the massive amphitheatre beneath the Chapel Crags of High Stile, and the other crossing the gill and ascending the flank of Dodd (often mistaken for Red Pike when seen from Buttermere) to the col with Red Pike.

Bleaberry Tarn is indeed a fine sanctuary, and an excellent place to put your feet up for a few minutes before resuming the ascent. All around, save on Red Pike's smooth cone tinted veraciously red by syenite, crags abound, jagged, steep and leaning on the tiny tarn, the grim, sculptured hallmark of volcanic activity. Facing you across the tarn is your irresistible objective, something that sooner or later drags you to your feet for the final assault.

Cross the outflow of the tarn and the remains of a wall to regain the main track. At the col ahead, it is an easy matter to canter out to Dodd and back before resuming the ascent which in its final stages steepens significantly and is ringed with outcrops of rock. The summit, among the finest in Lakeland for views, is marked by a large cairn, but is otherwise unadorned, and affords no shelter in poor weather.

DISTANCE: 2.7 kilometres (1.7 miles)
ASCENT: 645 metres (2115 feet)

The continuation to Starling Dodd is an uncomplicated affair. A few cairns indicate the general direction to take before leaving you to descend to a line of old fence-posts. On a clear day you can make directly for Starling Dodd, but in misty conditions it is worth remembering that though the fence-line takes you a little out of your way before turning through ninety degrees to aim for the minor top, Little Dodd, it is accompanied by a path which later, as it leaves the fence-line, skirts Little Dodd to gain a foothold on Starling Dodd. The summit, approached by grassy slopes, is marked by a moderate-sized cairn decorated with scrap iron from the old fence.

DISTANCE: 2 kilometres (1.25 miles)
ASCENT: 75 metres (245 feet)

Beyond Starling Dodd rises the grey, rocky top of Great Borne, easily reached on a clear path which eventually parallels a fence-line ascending to the summit – there is no need to cross the fence, despite a tempting stile. The summit of Great Borne has two tops, one on each side of the fence, but it is the southern one, marked by a trig point, which is the highest.

DISTANCE: 2 kilometres (1.25 miles)
ASCENT: 110 metres (360 feet)

On most days it is likely that you will find fifty walkers on the eastern end of this massive ridge for every one on the western end, and not surprisingly so. But the tranquillity and simplicity of pudding-shaped Starling Dodd and Great Borne are not to be scoffed at, and the return to Buttermere by descending steeply from Great Borne to Floutern Tarn, through the admittedly boggy headland of Mosedale, and by Scale Force along the shores of Crummock Water (Route 4.2 in reverse), is a rewarding experience.

Route 4.4 Red Pike, High Stile and High Crag from Buttermere This magnificent trinity of summits presents a marvellously sculptured and inspiring challenge. Denying Buttermere most of what little winter sunshine there is, the range is a masterpiece of natural architecture, but woefully brief and just a little betrayed by the comparatively innocuous rump firmly seated in the forests of Ennerdale. Even so, their traverse is a satisfying undertaking, especially from Buttermere, completed by a return along the south shore of Buttermere lake.

The start of the route coincides with Route 4.3 which should be followed to the summit of Red Pike.
DISTANCE: 2.7 kilometres (1.7 miles)
ASCENT: 645 metres (2115 feet)

From Red Pike head initially south and then south east to follow the rim of the immense corrie containing Bleaberry Tarn; in mist a line of old fence-posts acts as a good guide, but on a clear day it is especially rewarding to cross the top of Chapel Crags around the head of the corrie to gain the rough ground rising to High Stile, the highest summit of the range.
DISTANCE: 1.1 kilometres (0.7 miles)
ASCENT: 90 metres (295 feet)

The line of old fence-posts which led you to High Stile continues to High Crag, making navigation easy, but of

course they won't last for ever. The crossing however is simple, though the crags which here drop into Burtness Combe do so rather more severely than Chapel Crags on the other side of High Stile, calling for caution, particularly in winter conditions. The summit is marked by a cairn.

DISTANCE: 1.5 kilometres (0.9 miles)
ASCENT: 35 metres (115 feet)

Descend to Scarth Gap, carefully, by Route 4.5; the upper section of High Crag, known as Gamlin End, is notoriously loose.

Route 4.5 Scarth Gap and High Crag The ascents to Scarth Gap, both from Gatescarth and the Ennerdale Black Sail Youth Hostel are detailed in Route 4.6a.

The best line from the cairn at the summit of Scarth Gap (189134) is to turn right (if ascending from Gatescarth) or left (from Ennerdale) to pick up a path through the broken crags and loose scree of Seat, more or less following an old fence-line until, once beyond Seat, matters take a turn for the worse as you are faced with an unappetising grind up the steep scree slope that buttresses High Crag's eastern end; this is known as Gamlin End. The summit of High Crag is identified by a cairn near the old fence-line.

DISTANCE: (from Gatescarth) 3.4 kilometres (2.2 miles)
ASCENT: 630 metres (2065 feet)
DISTANCE: (from Ennerdale) 2.5 kilometres (1.6 miles)
ASCENT: 455 metres (1490 feet)

On the ascent from Gatescarth a short cut has been created alongside the intake wall, immediately beneath Seat. It follows a dilapidated wall to the old fence-line, joining it

◄ *Red Pike (Buttermere) in winter's raiment.*

Looking down Lingcomb Edge from Red Pike to Mellbreak and Loweswater. ►

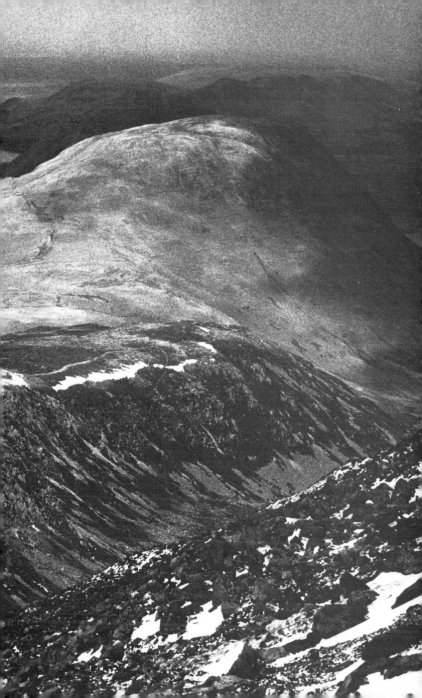

at the foot of Gamlin End. This route saves you a little distance, but none of the ascent. It also misses some of the panoramic advantages gained from the assault of Seat from Scarth Gap.

From High Crag the continuation to High Stile is easy, largely following the remains of the fence-line.
DISTANCE: 1.5 kilometres (0.9 miles)
ASCENT: 100 metres (330 feet)

Route 4.6 Hay Stacks Having announced my prejudice for this intriguing summit in the introduction to this section, I shall do no more other than to commend it to everyone, and point out how meaningless the arbitrary criteria of guide-book writers can become (600 metres in my case) when faced with a nonconformist like Hay Stacks.

4.6a From Gatescarth Two routes make for Hay Stacks from Gatescarth, one via Scarth Gap, the other by Warnscale Bottom, but it is worth remembering that the path through Burtness Wood from Buttermere along the southern shore of Buttermere lake (start as for Route 4.3) is also a delightful way of approaching Scarth Gap.

Leave Gatescarth farm (194150) along the track heading for Scarth Gap. Once beyond the limits of Buttermere, where the path through Burtness Wood arrives, the route ascends steeply for a while before easing to a more pleasant gradient for the final stretch to the large cairn marking the highest point of the pass. Here ascend a slanting rake, left, to a short downfall of scree, beyond which the path picks a way through a series of minor outcrops, some of which provide a scrambly alternative to the more conventional route. There is a good path all the way to the summit, marked by a cairn and an old fence-post, and if followed closely it will avoid any confusion that might arise in mist in this labyrinthine area of low craggy tops and shallow hollows. The summit, in any

Great Borne from Starling Dodd.

The summit of Great Borne.

Great Borne and the entrance to Ennerdale from Crag Fell.

event, is conspicuous by the proximity of a small tarn.
DISTANCE: 2.6 kilometres (1.6 miles)
ASCENT: 480 metres (1575 feet)

4.6b Via Warnscale Bottom From Gatescarth an equally
interesting alternative ascent starts through the narrow
declivity of Warnscale Bottom by a route originally constructed to serve the now disused Dubs quarry on the
southern slopes of Fleetwith Pike.

The track into Warnscale leaves Gatescarth 150 metres
east of the farm, just outside the intake wall, and the
passage into Warnscale is full of interest, especially as the
crags of Hay Stacks are approached. The main path
swings left to head for Dubs quarry, but may be left in
favour of another man-made track ascending in a series
of zig-zags beneath the crags. The easier way however
lies in following the main track to the quarry, where a
right turn and a short descent and re-ascent takes you on

Great Borne and the boggy headland of Mosedale.

to an elongated elevation of moorland, itself rising above
a further broad expanse of moorland stretching to distant
Brandreth, an area considered by M. J. B. Baddeley as
"specially designed to make one lose one's way in mist".
From the Dubs quarry a good path, soon joined by the
zig-zag path, skirts Blackbeck Tarn and Innominate Tarn
to the west (not named on the 1:50000 map) before
ascending easily to the top of Hay Stacks.
DISTANCE: 4 kilometres (2.5 miles)
ASCENT: 480 metres (1575 feet)

4.6c From Honister The ascent of Hay Stacks from
Honister, having the advantage of height, is an easy
undertaking, made easier by the arrow straight line of
the old tramway serving the Dubs quarry. The summit
however is obscured for most of the route, and when
finally seen, is rendered comparatively insignificant by
the higher fells which surround it.

Leave Honister, through the slate works at the top of the pass, and follow the sign-posted path to 'Dubs'; this is the same route as that for the ascent of Green Gable (Route 5.3). Once on the tramway follow it all the way to the quarry, ignoring the turning left towards Green Gable. At the quarry, join Route 4.6b, ascending through Warnscale Bottom, and wend a wandering way to the summit.

DISTANCE: 3.2 kilometres (2 miles)
ASCENT: 320 metres (1050 feet)

4.6d From Ennerdale (Black Sail Youth Hostel) It is not beyond the bounds of possibility simply to ascend directly up the fellside from the Black Sail Youth Hostel to the very summit of Hay Stacks, but to do so is to deny oneself the splendidly easy ascent along the perimeter fence of Ennerdale Forest to Scarth Gap.

The route is clear throughout, leaving the youth hostel

Mellbreak from the head of Mosedale.

on the main track through the valley, but quitting it as it enters the forest to ascend in the shade/shelter of the trees to within striking distance of the top of the pass, where you should join Route 4.6a for the rest of the ascent.

DISTANCE: 1.9 kilometres (1.2 miles)

ASCENT: 305 metres (1000 feet)

Route 4.7 Great Borne from Ennerdale Great Borne is probably more frequently ascended by walkers continuing westwards along the ridge from Red Pike, having dealt with Starling Dodd en route. The subsequent descent of Steel Brow (not named on the 1:50000 map) leads to the top of the Floutern Pass. Route 4.2 brings you up to this point from the direction of Buttermere, but the top of the pass may also be reached from Ennerdale by a shorter, more direct route.

Start at Whins farm (099167) and follow the grassy lane directly opposite the road junction to a gate in the intake wall, and there follow the path which ascends above Gill Beck (not named on the 1:50000 map) to the top of the pass, a boggy affair, crossed by a fence. Towering above you on the right is Steel Brow, and the fence-line ascending the fellside should be followed to the summit.

DISTANCE: 3.2 kilometres (2 miles)

ASCENT: 450 metres (1475 feet)

Section 5 – The Great Gable Group

	MAP REFERENCE	HEIGHT (m)	OS 1:50000 MAP
Great Gable	211103	899	89/90
Kirk Fell (South West Top)	195105	802	89/90
Green Gable	215107	801	89/90
Kirk Fell (North East Top)	199107	787	89/90
Brandreth	215119	715	89/90
Grey Knotts	217126	697	89/90

| Fleetwith Pike | 206142 | 648 | 89/90 |
| Base Brown | 225115 | 646 | 89/90 |

ROUTES

The summit of Great Gable, like those of all the central lakeland mountains, is owned by the National Trust. It was given to the Trust in 1923 by the Fell and Rock Climbing Club as a memorial to its members killed in the 1914–18 War, and it forms the centrepiece of the emblem of the Lake District National Park. Not by chance, as Walt Unsworth reminds us, was Great Gable chosen for such distinctions. Of all the Lakeland mountains "Great Gable represents the spirit of Lakeland. It is the quintessential fell; the one remembered when others are forgotten. Gable is as much romance as reality, like the Matterhorn, and just as the Matterhorn symbolizes the Alps so too Gable symbolizes Lakeland." Wainwright also chose his words carefully when he wrote: "The truth is, Great Gable casts a spell. It starts as an honourable adversary and becomes a friend."

Certainly it is a mountain held in great esteem and with much affection by rock climbers and hill-walkers alike. There is something here for everyone, unless you seek the very highest standards in modern rock gymnastics. And even then an occasional set-to with the crags of The Napes will remind you what these mountains are all about.

Green Gable by contrast boasts no such magnificence, daunted and over-shadowed by its higher sibling, to which it is joined tenuously by Windy Gap. Yet set it apart if you can, and give it some time instead of hastening across its narrow summit, and you will come to perceive that it does have a grandeur of its own. It also happens to be on two of the finest lines of ascent to Great Gable, those from the top of Honister Pass, and from Seathwaite via the hidden valley of Gillercomb.

At the northern end of this compact mountain stronghold, Honister Crag stands guardian of the high pass, Honister Hause (as it is properly known). The precipitous crags, from which the internationally famous Honister Green Slate is won, rise imperiously at the head of the Buttermere valley, culminating in the minor summit, Black Star, and the higher Fleetwith Pike.

Working conditions at the Honister Quarry, as elsewhere, were harsh and dangerous. Slate was brought down to the knapping sheds on hurdles or trail-barrows, which had two inclining handles (stangs) at the front between which the man would position himself, going, like a horse, before the weight. These contraptions weighed as much as eighty pounds, and it took the men half an hour of laborious effort to carry them back to the quarry, though the subsequent laden descent was often only a matter of minutes, depending on the skill, dexterity and good fortune of the man. Remarkable tales still abound of men of the 1860s: Samuel Trimmer, who once made fifteen journeys in a day for a bottle of rum and a small percentage of the slate he had sledged; and Joseph Clarke of Stonethwaite who made seventeen journeys, bringing down each time 640 pounds of slate, a total of 10,880 pounds, in one day. "His greatest day's work," writes Harriet Martineau, "was bringing 11,771 pounds; in how many journeys it is not remembered: but in fewer than seventeen." This dangerous method of obtaining slate was ended in 1881, when a gravitational railway, the course of which can still be traced, was introduced.

Quarry workers, like the dry-stone wallers, whose work still decorates the fellsides of Lakeland, often lived during the week in small huts on the hillsides, going home only from Saturday night until the following Monday morning, and while away, communicating with their wives by carrier pigeons.

At the other end of this range, and much less conspicuous than Fleetwith Pike and Honister Crag, except for travellers who venture into remote Wasdale, is Kirk Fell; a fine mountain, but sandwiched hopelessly between two giants, Great Gable and Pillar, and offering no easy ascent as Green Gable does, unless you consider a full frontal assault easy. In consequence, this grassy, twin-topped summit is frequently done less than justice.

Route 5.1 Fleetwith Pike from Gatescarth From Gatescarth, at the eastern end of Buttermere, Fleetwith Pike and the steep, dark profile of Honister Crag have an intimidating aura, and it is hard to accept that this way up is actually shorter than that from Honister; the fact that the ascent is almost twice as much has something to do with it. But neither approach will detain the experienced walker for more than half a day.

Start where the broad track into Warnscale Bottom leaves the Honister Pass road (196149), following this for a few strides until you can go left on a narrower path heading for Low Raven Crag (not named on the 1:50000 map) near the foot of which there is a conspicuous white cross to the memory of Fanny Mercer, who was accidentally killed here in 1887. Continue around Low Raven Crag and climb above it on a loose path to gain a grassy slope. Ascend this to rockier ground above, but don't be misled into thinking the knoll above you is the summit. The true summit lies a short distance further on and up.

DISTANCE: 1.2 kilometres (0.75 miles)
ASCENT: 525 metres (1720 feet)

Honister Crag, an imposing precipice, drops dramatically

northwards from the summit, calling for care in misty and winter conditions, while the minor summit, Black Star, lies a short distance east.

Route 5.2 Fleetwith Pike from Honister Pass The gaunt outline of Honister Crag is a familiar sight to motorists crossing from Borrowdale to Buttermere. It is a strong, striking and attractive downfall of naked ruggedness, with few equals in Lakeland, and commands attention.

The ascent from Honister, however, is far less imposing than such a bold front deserves. Leave the car park behind the youth hostel (225136) by a gate into the grounds of the slate works. Continue beyond the buildings to a sign pointing the way, left, to Great Gable and the disused Dubs quarry. Ignore this diversion and stay on the broad path for a while longer until it forks again. This time go left, ascending along the line of the old gravitational railway until this ends, and then continue on to the shoulder of Fleetwith Pike, making first for the minor summit, Black Star (212142 – not named on the 1:50000 map). The top of Fleetwith Pike lies a short distance west, and involves a little more ascent.

DISTANCE: 2 kilometres (1.25 miles)
ASCENT: 290 metres (950 feet)

Route 5.3 Grey Knotts, Brandreth and the Gables from Honister Pass There is little about either Grey Knotts or Brandreth to inspire the mind as they are encountered on this ascent from the top of the Honister Pass; their appeal lies in the rugged east face they present to the hanging valley of Gillercomb (see Route 5.4). Nor does the positive path from Honister, which makes determinedly for Green and Great Gable, do anything to encourage you to divert from it to take in these two knobbly summits. But they can be brought into a day's round with the Gables, even if only on the return journey.

Start from the car park at the rear of the youth hostel (225136), and pass through a gate into the grounds of

the Buttermere and Westmorland Green Slate Company.
Continue beyond the buildings and in a short distance
follow a path sign-posted 'Great Gable' and 'Dubs' –
Dubs is the quarry (210134) on the slopes of Fleetwith
Pike – ignoring a broad track going off to the right. Climb
steeply to gain the line of the old tramway used by the
quarry, and follow this until, as the gradient starts to
ease, you encounter an obvious path going left. This will
lead you at a gentle rate of ascent to Gillercomb Head at
215114, and will provide you with some excellent scenery,
encompassing Buttermere, Crummock Water, the High
Stile range, Ennerdale and Pillar.

To reach Grey Knotts from this path it is simply a
matter of choosing a point where you feel you can ascend
easily left through low outcrops and boulders to the
summit.

DISTANCE: 2.2 kilometres (1.4 miles)
ASCENT: 335 metres (1100 feet)

The top of Grey Knotts is in mist a confusion of rocky
tors and small lakes. A nearby ruined fence-line heading
north east will take you by a rough route back to the
Youth Hostel at Honister, if necessary, but take care not
to follow a second fence going south of east, which makes
for Gillercomb and a rather sudden drop!

To continue to Brandreth simply follow the fence-line,
roughly south.

DISTANCE: 0.8 kilometres (0.5 miles)
ASCENT: 30 metres (100 feet)

By following the fence-line south from Brandreth you
will come to Gillercomb Head, where you rejoin the direct
route from Honister.

From Gillercomb Head the way on to Green Gable is
clear enough, and near the summit joins Route 5.4, which
can then be followed to the top with its impressive view
of Ennerdale.

DISTANCE: (from Brandreth) 1.3 kilometres (0.8 miles)

ASCENT: (from Brandreth) 150 metres (490 feet)
DISTANCE: (by direct route from Honister) 4 kilometres
(2.5 miles)
ASCENT: (by direct route from Honister) 440 metres (1445
feet)

Along the direct route you will see, as you pass Brandreth,
a narrow path curving round beneath Green Gable and
the towering cliffs of Great Gable. This is Moses' Trod,
allegedly named after an illicit whisky distiller who used
it to transport his brew from Fleetwith to the inhabitants
of Wasdale. The route is very impressive, crossing the
very head of Ennerdale and making for Beck Head
(205107 – not named on the 1:50 000 map). The path
meets the north west shoulder of Great Gable a short
distance above Beck Head, and by using this route a steep
ascent can be made to the summit.
DISTANCE: 5 kilometres (3.1 miles)
ASCENT: 540 metres (1770 feet)

For an entertaining day, ascend from Honister direct to
Green Gable, then by Windy Gap to Great Gable. Leave
Great Gable by the north west ridge, as if en route for
Kirk Fell, and at Beck Head turn right along Moses'
Trod to Gillercomb Head, from where you can return to
Honister over Brandreth and Grey Knotts.

**Route 5.4 Base Brown and the Gables through Giller-
comb** Green Gable is a high mountain in its own right
which suffers by comparison with its mighty neighbour;
set apart, at the head of its own valley for example, it
would be a magnetic and deservedly popular objective.
Base Brown, far out on a limb overlooking the southern
terminus of Borrowdale, is even more often overlooked
and passed by. Yet here are three superbly-linked summits, each leading to something better, and more than
ample reward for a day's effort.
  Begin at Seathwaite Farm (235122) and leave through

The Taylorgill Force track from Seathwaite to Styhead crosses the southern slopes of Base Brown. Blencathra can be seen in the distance above the pastureland of Borrowdale.

the arch in the buildings on the right. Continue to a bridge across the River Derwent where a path to Taylorgill Force goes left through a gate. Ignore this path and keep ahead with the cascade of Sour Milk Gill spilling from the hanging valley of Gillercomb above. In a short distance cross the wall on your left by a slanting stile, and gain the path leading to and behind Seathwaite Slabs, an easy-angled rock slab suitable for novice rock climbers. The erosion control work which has been carried out here in recent years has been financed by the Lake District Landscape Fund, and should you wish to assist their work by sending a contribution, they can be contacted at Freepost, Ambleside, Cumbria, LA22 9BR.

At the top of Sour Milk Gill you encounter an impressive morainic ridge formed when the corrie glacier which gouged out the valley of Gillercomb finally lost its impetus

Sour Milk Gill above Seathwaite, in Borrowdale.   ▶

Raven Crag on Grey Knotts from the top of Sour Milk Gill.

and dumped its unwelcome load of boulder debris. This secret valley, quite unsuspected from Borrowdale, is a natural way to Green Gable. It is spacious, boggy and ringed with crags, and offers a mini-horseshoe over Base Brown, Green Gable, Brandreth and Grey Knotts to walkers who can find a way down the craggy shoulder of Grey Knotts.

A direct ascent of Base Brown may be made from the edge of Gillercomb, from where a faint path meanders upwards amid minor rock outcrops and buttresses. Easier is the path through Gillercomb which is level for part of the way before it climbs steeply to the col between Base Brown and Green Gable. The path to Base Brown from the col is indistinct and wet, but the summit is worth the detour.

DISTANCE: 2.7 kilometres (1.7 miles)
ASCENT: 515 metres (1690 feet)

Raven Crag (Grey Knotts) from the hanging valley, Gillercomb.

Continue to Green Gable by returning to the col and rejoin the main path which struggles upwards to the watershed to meet the path to Green Gable from Honister. Here go left to the fine summit of the lower Gable, which forms with Great Gable the headwall of Ennerdale.

DISTANCE: (from Base Brown) 1.3 kilometres (0.8 miles)
ASCENT: 195 metres (640 feet)
DISTANCE: (direct) 3 kilometres (1.9 miles)
ASCENT: 670 metres (2200 feet)

If the day is fine it would be a pity to hasten on indecently when Green Gable offers such tremendous views of the natural architecture which makes up Great Gable's northern face. Beyond rises the twin-topped Kirk Fell, and behind that Pillar and Scoat Fell.

The way on to Great Gable lies roughly south at first down a well-trodden and loose scree path to the top of

Looking across Windy Gap to Great Gable, and the Scafells.

Great and Green Gable from Seathwaite Fell.

This delightful study of Great Gable is taken across one of Seathwaite Fell's many tiny tarns, not over Sprinkling Tarn as might be supposed.

Windy Gap; this requires care at all times. From Windy Gap a cairned route ascends south west through a mêlée of boulders and collapsed rock faces to the summit.

DISTANCE: 0.6 kilometres (0.4 miles)
ASCENT: 150 metres (490 feet)

Route 5.5 Great Gable and Green Gable by Aaron Slack Aaron Slack is the shallow gully rising from Styhead valley between Great and Green Gable, which terminates rather abruptly at Windy Gap. There is some suggestion that it was used in Neolithic times as a link between stone axe factories in Langdale and coastal settlements on the West Cumberland plain, where the axes, rough cut in Langdale, were finished and polished.

'Slack' means scree, and on the face of it that sums up this route; it is also enclosed, claustrophobic, and has no views. On the plus side it is sheltered, you can't get lost in it, and the gradient and going not so bad as some would have you believe. That may not be enough to tempt you to ascend this way, but it is an admirable, safe and quick way down from the Gables in bad weather.

Leave Seathwaite, heading south, on the track between the farm buildings, and follow this to the old packhorse bridge, Stockley Bridge (234109). Cross the bridge and continue ahead through a gate, ignoring the track going left along the wall. Climb easily on an improved path to another gate before passing a small plantation on your right just above Taylorgill Force. Continue on a rough path parallel with Styhead Gill until you can cross it by a bridge.

This bridge may be reached from Seathwaite however by a route both shorter and more entertaining. Leave the farm through the arch in the buildings on the right, and continue to a bridge across the River Derwent. Here, with Sour Milk Gill tumbling down above you from the hidden valley of Gillercomb, go left at the first gate and cross a stretch of boggy ground. Keep going, the flanks of Base Brown rising above you, until you start to ascend through boulders to, of all things, a gate perched beneath the crags now pressing heavily on your right. Ahead, and at close range screened from walkers on the Stockley Bridge route, is one of Lakeland's most impressive sights, Taylorgill Force, a cascading mare's tail of surging water marking the downfall of Styhead Gill from its hanging valley into the main valley below. The way forward requires a little mild scrambling, but once above the force continue uneventfully to the bridge in parallel with the Stockley Bridge route on the other side of the river.

A short way ahead Styhead Tarn lies in one of the grandest, most satisfying settings in Lakeland. Not far from the bridge, and before Styhead Tarn is reached, bear right to start the climb into Aaron Slack. Initially the going is easier on the true left (your right) of the stream, later crossing and recrossing it before you reach the top.

Green Gable lies to the right, up a path of loose gravel, from Windy Gap.
DISTANCE: 4.2 kilometres (2.6 miles)
ASCENT: 670 metres (2200 feet)

Great Gable, a much rockier proposition, lies to the left.
DISTANCE: 4.4 kilometres (2.75 miles)
ASCENT: 770 metres (2525 feet)

Route 5.6 Great Gable from Seathwaite via Styhead

This has long been the tourist route to Great Gable, and is unlikely to cause anyone difficulty.

Reach Styhead by either of the lines described in Route 5.5 (by Stockley Bridge or Taylorgill Force), and at the Mountain Rescue stretcher box turn right, north west, to ascend a long, tedious, loose, rocky, well-cairned pathway, used by ponies in the days before degenerated to its

The south-west slope of Great Gable (Gavel Neese) rises to the Napes Ridge, beyond which lie Westmorland Crags.

Great Gable, from the Corridor Route to Scafell Pike.

present treadmill condition. The path wanders about a little, but is never in doubt, and leads you directly to the summit.

DISTANCE: 4.7 kilometres (2.9 miles)
ASCENT: 770 metres (2525 feet)

Route 5.7 Great Gable by the Napes The Napes look very much like an afterthought painted into the picture after it had been completed, almost as if in the Grand Design the scree- and debris-littered slopes were considered too barren, wanting for some of the cragginess that features on the mountain's northern face. They consist of a series of striking outcrops and rocky ridges projecting from the fellside overlooking the upper end of Wasdale, and, as a result, form a very airy situation. Once considered to be among the very finest rock-climbing grounds in England, the Napes have a unique attraction for walker and climber alike.

From Styhead a path slopes up across the fellside, between the direct line to Great Gable and the descent to Wasdale. You quickly reach the first major buttress, Kern Knotts, a massive downfall of boulders at its feet, on which the most conspicuous features are the two immense cracks that rent its face. That on the left, first ascended by Owen Glynne Jones in 1897, is known, not unexpectedly as Kern Knotts Crack, while the slightly more difficult right-hand crack became, paradoxically, Innominate Crack, but not for another twenty-five years.

Continue below Kern Knotts on a clear, but occasionally narrow, path until, around a corner the Napes come into view. The path you travel, known as the South Traverse, is part of a complete girdle of Great Gable, mostly justified by the Napes and the fine traverse around the head of Ennerdale on the other side of the mountain.

The first significant obstacle of any note is the crossing of the wide red screes of Great Hell Gate, beyond which the masterpiece of the Napes, Napes Needle, finally starts to stand out from the buttresses behind it, though as yet it hasn't quite assumed the form familiar in countless photographs. Continue on the South Traverse until slightly beyond the Needle, at which point you can enter Needle Gully and scramble up more scree to the foot of a towering buttress, Abbey Buttress, the platform at the bottom of which, known as the Dress Circle, forms an excellent vantage point for viewing and photographing the Needle. A short distance further on, across an awkward little slab with polished holds, an upthrust of rock provides another acceptable resting place looking back to the Needle and forward to Arrowhead Gully and its own rock feature, Sphinx Rock.

Walkers with scrambling skills will however prefer to ascend to the base of the Needle from below it and slightly to the right, and then to continue by a narrow gully with polished, but ample, holds to perform the feat of threading the Needle. The descent to Needle Gully can

Kirk Fell from the Napes Ridge.

be awkward, as can the initial ascent, if your figure is less than rakish or you are carrying a large rucksack.

Everything after the Needle is pure anticlimax. Sphinx Rock, also known as Cat Rock, is however worth a visit. It does resemble a cat, especially when viewed from below, but the profile claimed to look like a sphinx seems more like Geronimo to me. Perhaps, being so near to Arrowhead Gully, it should be renamed Apache Rock!

The South Traverse continues now to Beck Head, though walkers who enjoy paddling about on scree can ascend by Little Hell Gate to the top of the Napes Ridges and so on to the summit, turning Westmorland Crags, which guard the top of the mountain, on the left.

DISTANCE: (from Sty Head) 1 kilometre (0.6 miles)

ASCENT: 150 metres (490 feet)

Napes Needle: 'Threading the Needle' involves ascending by a steep and narrow gully (out of sight) to the narrow gap where the two rock-climbers are, then scrambling down the short wall beneath them to cross Needle Gully before reaching the sanctuary of the Dress Circle, or the small platform from which this picture was taken.

Kirk Fell and Great Gable peer over the grassy slopes of Lingmell.

Personally, I don't consider this an acceptable way to ascend Great Gable. But I do consider a day out to see Napes Needle well worthwhile – we don't always have to reach the summit of a mountain, do we?

Route 5.8 Great Gable from Wasdale It is not by chance that Great Gable figures as the centrepiece of the emblem of the Lake District National Park. Viewed from Wasdale the eye is unavoidably drawn to Gable, almost without a moment's glance for the other fine summits around; it is a commanding presence, and only the long journeys needed to get into Wasdale divert the feet of most walkers to ascents from Seathwaite or Honister.

5.8a By Sty Head The long ascent to Sty Head seems to be taking you out of your way, moving from the south west of the mountain to the south east before starting to get to grips with it. The route however is pleasant, a little loose and slippery in places and rocky near the top, though it promises much without ever quite fulfilling the promise.

Kirk Fell and Great Gable from Yewbarrow.

Kirk Fell from Hay Stacks.

Mist covered Great Gable and Green Gable rise at the head of Ennerdale. ▶

Leave Wasdale along the lane past the hotel, as if heading for the Black Sail Pass, but just as you start to climb to enter Mosedale turn right towards Burnthwaite Farm, crossing a stream by many small wooden foot bridges before arriving at a larger bridge spanning Gable Beck at 199093. Continue ahead on a track which parallels Lingmell Beck and passes beneath the stark outline of the Great Napes Buttresses, until you arrive at the Mountain Rescue stretcher box at Sty Head. Here join Route 5.6 for the final steep section to the summit.

DISTANCE: 4.3 kilometres (2.7 miles)
ASCENT: 820 metres (2690 feet)

5.8b By Beck Head The Beck Head route is more direct than that by Sty Head, but is a little two-faced, luring you up pleasant grassy slopes, but then, once you have committed yourself, suddenly turning to loose scree and shattered rock outcrops before you gain the summit.

Leave the Sty Head route at the wooden bridge (199093), and follow a conspicuous rising track on the left, this is Moses' Trod. Half way up this ascent it is possible to keep ahead, and up, to make directly for the summit, but unless you enjoy the treadmill of scree slopes, I don't recommend it. Better, and more sensible, is to stay with Moses' Trod to Beck Head, and to keep high on that track (rather than descend to the col) in order to gain Gable's north west ridge. Follow the well-worn trail through the boulder slopes that comprise the north west ridge, ending only a short distance from the summit cairn, perched on top of a rock upthrust.

DISTANCE: 3.4 kilometres (2.1 miles)
ASCENT: 820 metres (2690 feet)

The two Gables at the very head of Ennerdale. ▶

Great Gable across Wastwater, the classic symbol of Lakeland. ▶ ▶

Route 5.9 Kirk Fell from Wasdale Between two such immense geological masterpieces as Great Gable and Pillar the mere detail of Kirk Fell tends to be overlooked, an insignificant grassy dome, strenuous in ascent, and offering little to compare with its neighbours. But tackle this underrated eruption on a Bank Holiday, when the skyline all around is dotted with lines of little Indians, and, like me, you will suddenly realise an unsuspected potential. And if you don't fancy the steep ascents an approach from Wasdale requires, try coming at it from Honister, by Moses' Trod to Beck Head, crossing the mountain to the top of the Black Sail Pass and returning by the linking traverse to Beck Head.

Kirk Fell has two distinct summits – south west, the highest, and north east, and with more than thirty metres of re-ascent between them, both fall within the criteria I have used for inclusion in the Tables of this book. So if

Grey Knotts from Moses' Trod.

you're a list ticker you need to visit them both! Three ascents are available from Wasdale Head, all of them leaving the valley along the lane from the hotel, as if heading for the Black Sail Pass – which is one of the options.

5.9a Direct Given that the shortest distance between two points is a straight line, this route could never be accused of lacking geometrical precision, for it does just that. It will appeal only to walkers who have something to prove, and the strongest of the strong.

Pursue the path to Black Sail until clear of the intake wall, at a gate, from where the route takes off, straight up the fellside, and only ceases to be a prominent path as you traverse a couple of natural dykes near the south west summit, by which time the summit cairn is in view.

DISTANCE: 1.8 kilometres (1.1 miles)
ASCENT: 720 metres (2360 feet)

Wainwright, never stuck for words, describes this ascent as "a relentless and unremitting treadmill, a turf-clutching crawl", which seems about right. I've seen people on it, and they didn't look at all happy, but it does make for a speedy descent to Wasdale in the event of a sudden adverse change in the weather. Even then, when you finally hit bottom your legs will feel like scrambled black puddings.

The south west summit has two cairns, one, the more northerly, close by an old fence-line. Find the fence-line and follow it unerringly to the north east summit, by-passing two small tarns en route, it is a totally safe guide in mist, continuing on to Beck Head.

DISTANCE: 0.5 kilometres (0.3 miles)
ASCENT: 36 metres (120 feet)

5.9b By Black Sail Pass The ascent by the Black Sail Pass is a much easier proposition, and passes unevent-fully through Mosedale before ascending right to cross

Gatherstone Beck (not named on the 1:50 000 map) for the pull, by a loose path, to the pass.

From the top of the pass ascend east of south up a path of scree to tangle with a delightful downfall of rocky ledges and outcrops that at first sight appear quite daunting. But good sense and a modicum of caution will soon have you on to easier ground above, where the fence-line re-appears and takes you straight to the south west summit.

DISTANCE: 4.3 kilometres (2.7 miles)
ASCENT: 720 metres (2360 feet)

5.9c By Beck Head Beck Head lies between Kirk Fell and Great Gable, and may be reached from Wasdale by taking the track, right, near the start of the Black Sail

Fleetwith Pike and Dubs Quarry.

path heading for Styhead. Cross a wooden bridge (199093) where Gable Beck (not named on the 1:50 000 map) flows to Lingmell Beck, and ascend, left, on a conspicuous, loose path, starting at a large cairn near the bridge. This ascent takes you directly to Beck Head, a broad col between Kirk Fell on your left and Gable on the right, and containing two small tarns. The remains of a fence-line cross the col, and can be followed left and upwards to Kirk Fell's north east summit. Don't follow the fence too literally on the col, it passes through the middle of Beck Head Tarn!

The north east summit is marked by a cairn perched on top of a rocky outcrop, with the fence-line passing nearby.

DISTANCE: 3.5 kilometres (2.2 miles)
ASCENT: 705 metres (2310 feet)

Continue to the higher, south west summit by a direct line (in good weather) passing between the two tarns that make up Kirkfell Tarn, or by following the fence-line; but note that the fence passes a few metres to the north of the highest point.

DISTANCE: 0.5 kilometres (0.3 miles)
ASCENT: 51 metres (167 feet)

Section 6 – The Pillar Group

	MAP REFERENCE	HEIGHT (m)	OS 1:50 000 MAP
Pillar	171121	892	89/90
Scoat Fell (Little Scoat Fell)	160114	841	89
Unnamed Summit (Top of Black Crag)	166117	828	89
Red Pike	165106	826	89
Steeple	157117	819	89
Haycock	145107	797	89
Seatallan	140084	692	89

Caw Fell	132110	690c	89
Iron Crag	123119	642	89
Yewbarrow	173085	628	89/90
Yewbarrow – North East Top (Stirrup Crag)	176092	616	89/90
Lank Rigg	092119	541	89
Crag Fell	097144	523	89
Grike	086141	486	89

ROUTES

6.1   Pillar from Wasdale
6.2   Pillar from Ennerdale
6.3   Yewbarrow, Red Pike, Scoat Fell from Wasdale
6.4   Seatallan and Haycock from Greendale
6.5   Haycock and Scoat Fell by Nether Beck
6.6   Iron Crag and Caw Fell across Kinniside Common

The vast tract of countryside over which I have ordained the singular mountain, Pillar, to reign, is more properly titled Copeland Forest: it is only because the forest was of much larger dimension than the compass of the Pillar group of fells, extending from the Esk to the Derwent and westwards to the Irish Sea, that I have introduced a modern description. The name derives from the Norse, *Kaupa-land*, a 'bought' land, as distinct from one inherited, and suggests that it was the influence of Scandinavian settlers which brought the land into cultivation and habitable condition, though the identity of the original vendor and buyer is now lost.

Copeland was a private forest, under the Barony of Copeland, but a forest only in a legal sense, and not necessarily totally covered with trees. Like many others, it was a region where the Forest Laws, introduced by the Normans, prevailed probably until the early thirteenth century to protect the owner who desired to hunt game, against the interests of the local population who wished only to enclose and improve the land for agricultural use. Gradually however as the demand for land became greater, the forests were reduced, leaving only the fast-nesses of the mountains to serve the hunt, a process completed in Copeland around 1578, by which time the hunting preserve was restricted to upper Ennerdale. Indeed, one of the last refuges of red deer in this region was the fellside south of Ennerdale Water now called 'The Side', where in 1675, according to Edmund Sandford, in *A cursory relation of all the Antiquities and Families in Cumberland*, "there is red deer, and Hartts and Staggs as great as in any part of England".

For the fell wanderer however most of the interest of this exquisite wedge of Lakeland is confined to the eastern end, around Pillar, and principally accessible from Wasdale Head. In the routes that follow I have described the pleasures and delights of each summit as well as the valleys of Mosedale, Nether Beck and Greendale. My only regret is that afforestation work in Ennerdale makes it, as yet, an unattractive by-way to the fells of the Pillar group, though those sentiments do not apply to any walk confined to the shores of Ennerdale Water or along the length of the valley to the Black Sail Youth Hostel.

South of Ennerdale Water, and west of the high fells, lies a tantalising, lonely country, unvisited by most walkers, scarcely explored. Here Stockdale Moor rises from the mantle of dark coniferous forest in the Bleng valley, a region liberally strewn with evidence, faint though it may seem to the superficial glance, of prehistoric settlements. Stone cairns occur by the hundred, while walled enclosures, hut circles and the traceable layout of fields all point to early settlements. Little datable evidence has yet been found, making this moorland area a potential paradise for the archaeologist. As a result, it is not too fanciful to envisage the moor inhabited in turn by Bronze Age farmers, Celtic-speaking Britons, tenth-century Viking shepherds, and farmers from the Cumberland plain during the fourteenth and fifteenth centuries exploiting the grazing land of the high fells during summer months. It is all a fascinating, remarkable region.

Route 6.1 Pillar from Wasdale Pillar, quite rightly, is an immensely popular summit, not only because of its commanding position at the head of Mosedale, and for that matter much of Ennerdale until Great Gable comes into view, but also for the impressive fang of rock, Pillar Rock, on its steep north face.

From Wasdale Head the route to the Black Sail Pass, the key to this ascent, is sign-posted through the buildings near the hotel. Take care on the broad path that follows not to be misled into crossing the attractive stone bridge near Row Head farm (not named on the 1:50000 map), which will only lead you into Mosedale, on completely the wrong side of Mosedale Beck. By continuing ahead you will come eventually to the obvious start of the route to the Black Sail Pass, a longish but uncomplicated ascent.

As you gaze at Pillar from the valley the most conspicu-

Pillar rises in the distance at the head of Mosedale, the long screes leading to Wind Gap clearly visible. The intervening slope is that of Lingmell.

ous feature is the massively long scree run descending from Wind Gap, to the south west of the mountain. Stalwarts, for want of a better expression, will find this line of ascent, which diverts from the main valley path at a cairn, before the intake wall is reached, an excruciating test of their stamina, one to which I strongly counsel aversion. I fail to see why anyone would want to trudge wearily up this treadmill when you can recourse to an infinitely gentler and sedate plod to the top of the Black Sail Pass. Here a line of old fence-posts leads you by a series of grassy and rocky rises – a fine ridge with exhilarating views – to the bald dome of Pillar's summit; an excellent walk. The highest point is marked by a trig point and shelter cairn.

DISTANCE: 5.7 kilometres (3.6 miles)

ASCENT: 810 metres (2655 feet)

The long scree run leading to Wind Gap is seen in this distant picture of (most of) the Mosedale Horseshoe.

Pillar, seen from Red Pike (Buttermere). Pillar Rock, not well seen from this angle, occupies the dark mass beneath the summit.

The ascent by the Black Sail Pass has distinct advantages over the Wind Gap route. It allows you to take in the minor top, Looking Stead, en route, which is an excellent vantage point for Ennerdale and leads on to the High Level Route to Pillar Rock, Robinson's Traverse. No walker should delay for too long the ascent of Pillar by this remarkable route. Discovered by J. W. Robinson, a pioneer of rock-climbing, the High Level Route leaves the east ridge of Pillar immediately after Looking Stead and traverses below the crags of Green Cove and Hind Cove (not identified on the 1:50 000 map) to the prominent cairn built in memory of Robinson. At the cairn the full splendour of Pillar Rock suddenly bursts into view. There is about it an arrogant, unremitting challenge that makes me, for one, relive my better moments with rock and rope.

The daunting crags of Pillar Rock: the extension on the right is Pisgah, separated from Pillar Rock by the Jordan Gap.

The profile of the Rock is carved in three stages. The right hand, its rugged wall plunging vertically into Pillar Cove, is Low Man, while immediately above it rises the knuckled top of High Man, the highest point of the Rock. Moving left there comes a deep notch, Jordan Gap, before the final piece of rock architecture, Pisgah, adjoining the main fell by an easy ridge. As if that isn't enough, the foreground is uniquely compromised by yet another huge crag, the Shamrock, half obscuring Pillar Rock but giving a tremendous perspective to the whole massive construction.

For the walker the bad news is that virtually the whole of this geological contrivance is out of bounds. So complex and dangerous are the approaches, all of which lead into increasing difficulty, that the only wise thing to do is stare in awe and admiration, and press on. Beyond Robinson's

Cairn the path dips to an easy low rock ridge which then takes you to the start of an exciting traverse, a broad ledge, high on Shamrock, known as the Shamrock Traverse, though without undue difficulty. Eventually you arrive tantalisingly close to Pisgah, which by now has lost all of its dramatic form, though the whole situation, high on a rugged fellside with enormous precipices all around, is pure magic. Linger for a while by all means, but sooner or later you must turn to tackle the final, steep pull, a well-trodden path, to the summit, by which (compared with what has just preceded it) everyone will be thoroughly underwhelmed. The distance and ascent are little more than by the ridge; in any case it is the spectating which will consume most of your time.

Route 6.2 Pillar from Ennerdale Pillar displays a much more dramatic face to Ennerdale than to Wasdale, but afforestation in the valley now makes a direct assault if

The bald dome of Pillar looms over the intermediate unnamed summit (Top of Black Crag).

not impossible, at least unrealistic. People still do struggle through the debris of tree felling operations that have obscured the former paths, but it's not much fun. For this reason I am opting to omit all but one ascent from this direction. A sad state of affairs, let us hope that if I revise this book some years hence I can include some better news.

My one option starts at the Black Sail Youth Hostel, to which you will already have had quite a walk, first along the shores of Ennerdale Water and then through the forest itself from Bowness Knott (110154), beyond which you cannot drive. Alternatively, you can of course reach the youth hostel from Gatescarth over Scarth Gap.

Leave the youth hostel by the well-trodden Black Sail Pass route, pursuing the course of Sail Beck (not named on the 1:50000 map) which gathers its water from the slopes of Kirk Fell above. At the top of the pass join Route 6.1 either to reach Pillar by the ridge route, safe and with excellent views, or by Robinson's Traverse, dramatic, exciting, breathtaking, etc., etc.

DISTANCE: 3.3 kilometres (2 miles) from Black Sail Youth Hostel
ASCENT: 600 metres (1968 feet)

Route 6.3 Yewbarrow, Red Pike and Scoat Fell from Wasdale No ascent of Yewbarrow is easy, either of line or effort. Yet it is a fell everyone should climb, an elongated, triple-topped ridge with splendid views especially of the Scafells and Wastwater; an energetic start or a fitting conclusion to a day among the exquisite fells of the Pillar range.

Start from the car park at Overbeck Bridge (168068), and ascend through bracken to a gate at the foot of the long wall which can be seen charging up the early slopes of Yewbarrow. Pass through the gate and follow a clear path alongside the wall until, near the bottom of the towering crags above, prominent among which is the pinnacle of Bell Rib, you can follow a path going left to the foot of a scree runnel alongside another steep cliff, Dropping Crag. Ascend the rough, grassy fellside on the right of the scree shoot until you are forced on to or across it, and continue laboriously to an open slope allowing you finally to work a way to the right to gain the ridge of Yewbarrow directly above Bell Rib, at a huge cleft, Great Door. Take a well-earned rest!

The remainder of the ascent to the top of Yewbarrow follows a clear path, and crosses first a minor top, Long Crag, before reaching the cairn on the highest point.

DISTANCE: 1.9 kilometres (1.2 miles)
ASCENT: 560 metres (1835 feet)

Continue pleasantly along the summit ridge to gain the North East Top, Stirrup Crag, and then prepare for a dramatic descent to Dore Head. The route is never in doubt, but walkers of a timid disposition may not take too kindly to Stirrup Crag's scrambly northern rampart. Taken sensibly however the descent need alarm no one, and it can be good fun, though it is undoubtedly better in ascent. Posteriors to the fore, if prudence dictates.

Dore Head can also be reached by pursuing the Mosedale path (sign-posted) from Wasdale Head to the grassy slopes beyond the debris cascading from Stirrup Crag, and then ascending steeply from there (though Heaven knows why anyone would want to!). Beyond this broad col an excellent path continues to the summit of Red Pike.

DISTANCE: 2.7 kilometres (1.7 miles)
ASCENT: 370 metres (1215 feet)

To continue to Scoat Fell (actually Little Scoat Fell) descend from Red Pike to a more prominent path than that on the summit ridge of the fell, and maintain a direct line from the intervening depression, ignoring a clear track that you will see shooting off to the right – this leads to the unnamed summit south west of Pillar. The highest point of Scoat Fell is directly beneath the cairn built on

Scoat Fell and Steeple from the unnamed summit (Top of Black Crag).

top of the high wall across the summit plateau, a unique summit cairn.

DISTANCE: 1 kilometre (0.6 miles)
ASCENT: 75 metres (245 feet)

From the top of Scoat Fell, a fairly uninteresting affair were it not for the impressive drop to the north into Mirk Cove (not named on the 1:50000 map), you can reach Pillar by following the wall, right (north east), until it abruptly ends, and then crossing, on a good path, the unnamed summit before a loose descent to a remarkable, airy col, Wind Gap, followed by an equally loose assault on the final slopes of Pillar itself.

Also within easy reach is Steeple, an awe-inspiring tribute to the Great Geological Architect. On the north side of the wall, easy going leads, left, to a cairn marking the start of the descent to the col with Steeple, from

where you can scamper delightfully to the cairned summit perched on the very edge of Mirk Cove, with the bald dome of Pillar rising in the distance.

Route 6.4 Seatallan and Haycock from Greendale

Seatallan is not a summit that every walker in Lakeland could place immediately. It is tucked away quietly to the north of Nether Wasdale, and invariably passed unnoticed by the mass of visitors. True, there are better things further east in the valley, but Seatallan deserves the occasional visit, and makes a pleasant, uncomplicated start to a superb round of the fells taking in Haycock, Scoat Fell, Red Pike and Yewbarrow.

Start from Greendale (144056) and take the obvious track on the true left bank of the gill issuing from Green-dale Tarn and the lower slopes of Seatallan (Greendale Gill – not named on the 1:50 000 map). The path soon enters a narrow ravine into which spill many gills, hence the name Tongues Gills, and continues a pleasant line to Greendale Tarn. It is possible to cross Greendale Gill once the gradient starts to ease, but I find it no less rewarding to keep on to the tarn which reposes peacefully beneath the rugged face of Middle Fell to the east.

From the tarn take a trackless route, north west, to gain the slopes of Seatallan, and an easy, rising approach to the summit, marked by a trig.

DISTANCE: 3 kilometres (1.9 miles)
ASCENT: 615 metres (2015 feet)

Note, if you only want a short walk, that there is an excellent, slightly longer, return route to Greendale over Middle Fell. Descend south of east from Seatallan to the

The unnamed summit (Top of Black Crag) against a background of Scoat
▲ *Fell and Steeple.*

◄ *Steeple.*

The eastern face of Red Pike (Wasdale): the summit in the left background is Scafell.

boggy col north of Greendale Tarn where you will pick up a path leading on to the northern end of Middle Fell. The path across Middle Fell is cairned all the way, and returns you to the vicinity of Tongues Gills.

DISTANCE: 3.7 kilometres (2.3 miles)
ASCENT: 115 metres (380 feet)

For Haycock the route is virtually trackless, and steep in descent. Move north-eastward along the edge of the north-facing slopes of Seatallan until you can find a comfortable way down to the col, shortly before which you will start to pick up a path. Once across the col, which is marshy, the path seems to forget its purpose for a while, wandering aimlessly round to the south-eastern corner of Haycock before making any attempt to ascend to the summit. Scramblers will find a more direct line from the col entertaining.

The summit of Haycock is rocky and adorned with a number of cairns all vying for the distinction enjoyed by the highest point on the north side of the wall traversing the top roughly from east to west.

DISTANCE: 2.6 kilometres (1.6 miles)
ASCENT: 300 metres (985 feet)

The wall across the summit of Haycock leads east directly to Scoat Fell.

DISTANCE: 1.7 kilometres (1 mile)
ASCENT: 135 metres (440 feet)

Westward, the wall canters over Little Gowder Crag to Caw Fell.

DISTANCE: 1.5 kilometres (0.9 miles)
ASCENT: 15 metres (50 feet)

From Greendale Tarn a boggy and trackless line north-wards to the col between Seatallan and Middle Fell will bring you to a good path high above Nether Beck, and on to the col beneath Haycock, so by-passing Seatallan altogether.

Route 6.5 Haycock and Scoat Fell by Nether Beck

The valley of Nether Beck, extending northwards from Wasdale, is the perfect place to rest a weary soul, a gentle, curving glen of bright green pastures and rippling streams.

Near Netherbeck Bridge (161066 – not named on the 1:50000 map) there is a small lay-by which will take a few cars, and from here you can head directly into the valley. The first few hundred metres are wet, until you reach a broad path which actually starts 300 metres west of the parking spot. Once on the path, continue at a leisurely pace, well into the valley. Middle Fell is the high crag on your left, and later Seatallan appears standing rather further back, as if distancing itself from mundane objects like pedestrians.

Towards the head of the valley the good path ends and divides. By going right, you cross Nether Beck and ascend a little to Scoat Tarn, a most attractive setting, beyond which an indistinct path follows what remains of an old fence-line to the col between Red Pike and Scoat Fell (Little Scoat Fell), from where the latter summit is easily attained.

DISTANCE: 6 kilometres (3.75 miles)
ASCENT: 770 metres (2525 feet)

By heading left at the fork you gain a shallow hanging valley, where a good path now reappears. Follow this to the col between Haycock and Great Scoat Fell, from where Haycock is easily reached by ascending, left, following the wall which crosses all these fells, and is a safe guide in mist.

DISTANCE: 5.5 kilometres (3.4 miles)
ASCENT: 725 metres (2380 feet)

From the col you may also ascend right, alongside the wall, first over Great Scoat Fell, and so to Little Scoat Fell, which is the highest point of the Scoat Fell complex.

DISTANCE: 6.2 kilometres (3.9 miles)
ASCENT: 770 metres (2525 feet)

Great Scoat Fell is only greater than Little Scoat Fell in bulk; Little Scoat Fell, which bears the banner of Scoat Fell, is greater in height! (Another example of the topsy-turvy situation found in Scotland on Aonach Beag and Aonach Mhor, and in Wales on Bera Mawr and Bera Bach.)

For a most pleasurable day's walking, try using Nether Beck to gain Scoat Fell by Haycock col, visiting Steeple and continuing to Pillar (with a short excursion down Pillar's north west ridge to have a look at Pillar Rock), before returning to conquer Red Pike and Yewbarrow.

DISTANCE: 16 kilometres (10 miles)
ASCENT: 1220 metres (4000 feet)

Scoat Fell and Steeple from Haycock.

Descending from Haycock to distant Caw Fell.

Haycock, from the summit of Seatallan.

Haycock

Seatallan, an infrequently-visited summit, viewed from the slopes of Haycock.

On the banks of Greendale Tarn. The snowy summits beyond the col are Haycock and Scoat Fell.

Middle Fell and Greendale Tarn. ►

Route 6.6 Iron Crag and Caw Fell across Kinniside Common Kinniside Common, like many parts of the West Cumberland plain, features prominently in man's pre-history, with many scattered clusters of cairns on scarcely explored sites assuming a familiar prehistoric pattern on the landscape. It is a remote region of wild moorland and forest, of easy walking and gentle rises, and a perfect arena for walkers in search of solitude. Like the rounded fells of Loweswater to the north, the summits of Kinniside Common are seldom visited, and provide excellent alternatives to higher summits suffering from Bank Holiday fever and other such fell-walking maladies.

Iron Crag will be quite sufficient objective from the Coldfell road, and may be reached by two routes; the extension to Caw Fell is an optional extra, but can add just a little too much to the day.

6.6a From Scaly Moss Begin at a bridleway sign-posted to Red Beck (which flows into Ennerdale Water east of Crag Fell). This leaves the fell road at 061137, follow it to a stile (next to a gate) facilitating entry into a forest. The bridleway is an old mine road across the fells to the slopes above Ennerdale. Continue through the forest, the track now littered with the debris of many storms, until, at a clearing, you encounter another gate. Do not tackle this gate, but move right and then left to stay within the forest boundary fence, heading for the summit, now in view, of Grike, a lonely Kinniside outpost, but one with excellent views.

To reach Grike you will need to leave the mine road either at its highest point, or earlier, where a fence ascends

---

Stirrup Crag, the north-east top of Yewbarrow towers above Mosedale. ▲

Stirrup Crag, Yewbarrow's north-east top from Dore Head. The route through the upper rock section is far less difficult than it seems. ▶

the fellside at right angles to the track. The fence does not cross the top of the fell, which is marked by a large cairn, an equally large shelter-cairn, and a shelter, all quite splendid.

Move right from the summit, as if returning to the mine road, but stay on the north side of the fence, and head for the col with the next summit, Crag Fell. An intersecting fence at the col is crossed by a stile. The ground here is a little boggy, but not a problem. Like Grike, Crag Fell, its summit marked by a solitary cairn, is a restful place, and has a magnificent view of the whole length of Ennerdale from Bowness Knott to Hay Stacks.

Descend south east from the top of Crag Fell to rejoin the mine road, but on doing so leave it immediately and pick up a path through a fire break to reach a stile (near a gate) which, at last, gets you on to the lower slopes of Iron Crag. A wall can now be followed all the way to the summit, the highest point of which, at the southern end of the long summit plateau, is marked by a cairn. The trig station suggested by some maps does not exist.

DISTANCE: 7.7 kilometres (4.8 miles) including Grike and Crag Fell

ASCENT: 560 metres (1835 feet)

Continue to Caw Fell simply by following the wall, turning left (east) when it does to reach the top of the fell.

DISTANCE: 1.6 kilometres (1 mile)

ASCENT: 110 metres (360 feet)

6.6b Along the River Calder and Whoap Beck Bearing its name from birth, the River Calder, a mere stream at its source between the minor summit of Crag Fell and Whoap, is assisted within only a few kilometres by a whole host of gills and becks with splendid names – Caplecrag Beck, Latterbarrow Beck, Ya Gill, Bomery Gill, Stinking Gill, and Whoap Beck. It is by a good path along the banks of Whoap Beck that an alternative ascent to Iron Crag may be made.

Yewbarrow.

Just south of Blakeley Raise, the Coldfell road turns sharply, and from here (067130) a Land-Rover track heads east to meet the Calder. A better track materialises here, and continues to cross the Calder near its source before pursuing the course of Whoap Beck to the col between Whoap and one of the loneliest summits in Lakeland, Lank Rigg.

An ascent of Lank Rigg from the col is easily undertaken, up a trackless fellside to a trig pillar and cairn. Return to the col and plod up the slopes of Whoap, a minor top with an unmarked summit. Continue, north of east, to meet the wall ascending Iron Crag, and follow this to the summit.

DISTANCE: 8 kilometres (5 miles) including Lank Rigg
ASCENT: 535 metres (1755 feet)

There are few positively identifiable features in this remote region, and walkers intent on visiting the tops would be well advised to wait for a clear day.

Section 7 – The Scafells

	MAP REFERENCE	HEIGHT (m)	OS 1:50 000 MAP
Scafell Pike	215072	978	89/90
Scafell	207065	964	89/90
Ill Crag	223073	935	89/90
Broad Crag	218076	934	89/90
Great End	227084	910	89/90
Lingmell	209082	800c	89/90
Slight Side	210050	762	89/90
Seathwaite Fell	227097	632	89/90
Illgill Head	169049	609	89

ROUTES
7.1 Scafell Pike from Seathwaite
7.2 Scafell Pike from Langdale
7.3 Scafell Pike from Eskdale
7.4 Scafell Pike from Wasdale
7.5 Scafell from Wasdale
7.6 Scafell from Eskdale over Slight Side
7.7 Scafell from Eskdale by Cam Spout
7.8 Scafell Pike and Scafell across Mickledore
7.9 Illgill Head and Whin Rigg
7.10 Lingmell from Seathwaite
7.11 Lingmell from Wasdale
7.12 Great End from Langdale
7.13 Great End from Seathwaite
7.14 Seathwaite Fell from Seathwaite

Unlike the highest mountains of Scotland, Wales, Eire and Northern Ireland, England's most noble rock prefers a sheltered existence, hiding discreetly behind a fringe of gallant outliers. Such glimpses as the motorist travelling around Lakeland will see are but brief and distant, while the walker must travel some way before the true scale of the mountain can be appreciated. As you ramble around its base you recognise that here is something special, but infuriatingly it remains hidden. Only at the expense of a good deal of energy do you start to get some idea that Scafell Pike, and, to be fair, its attendants, stand well in the company of the best in Britain. From Crinkle Crags or Bowfell you have a fine profile, while the view from the Roman fort at Hard Knott realigns the perspective and composes a more rugged, brooding picture. Walkers in Wasdale, from where begins the shortest ascent, must however content themselves with an initially poor impression of these much-loved mountains, Scafell Pike not having even so much as a toehold in the valley, its western slope being brought neatly to a point by the combined efforts of Scafell and Lingmell long before it bottoms out.

The core of the region is a long, excruciatingly rugged sequence of summits rising in the south from the diminutive Slight Side, across the Mickledore-hyphenated Scafell and Scafell Pike, the guardians of the northern approaches Broad Crag and Ill Crag – together with Scafell Pike making up the three Scafell Pikes – and so on to the appropriately-named Great End, sentinel of Borrowdale. A complete traverse from Wha House in Eskdale to Seathwaite in Borrowdale sure beats the hell out of gardening, watching television, washing the car, walking the dog, and all the countless weekend duties that so bedevil domestic life these days.

The whole of this high land is dominated by ankle-twisting boulders of every shape and size, and it is a test of strength to reach the highest point from any direction. Scafell Pike and its scarcely inferior sibling Scafell are not only fittingly massive and complicated but dangerously so as well. Both mountains are edged with the most severe of crags, around which even the easy ways are formidable. But I have no wish to deny anyone the pleasure of the ascent, only a desire to see them accomplish it in safety and with the knowledge that they conquered the King of Mountains aware of the consequences of getting it wrong.

Scafell Pike has none of the elegant simplicity of line of Great Gable, Skiddaw or Bowfell, and its major crags, Esk Buttress, concealed high in Upper Eskdale and Pikes

Crag, vastly overshadowed by the mighty precipices of Scafell Crag across the gulf of Hollow Stones, were for a long time ignored by the rock-climbing fraternity. Scafell by comparison knew no such neglect, having captured the imaginations of the pioneers of the Golden Age of rock-climbing long before their attention was drawn to the higher mountain. Alas for the walker, Scafell from Scafell Pike can be forbidden territory, as anyone who has gazed across the grassy oasis of Mickledore at the towering severity of Scafell Crag or the beer-belly bulges of East Buttress will know. Much as one might wish for an easy link between the two, none exists, and only those with a good measure of self-discipline and mountaineering expertise tend to complete the traverse. The connection, tenuous as it is, is of such complexity that I have seen fit in the routes that follow to award it its own separate description. But if you don't feel up to tackling Scafell from Scafell Pike, don't despair, there are other ways, but you must at least visit Mickledore, if only to amuse yourself watching the antics, particularly on Broad Stand, of walkers who should have known better.

Lying at the extremities, Great End and Slight Side are undeservedly neglected, while Lingmell, a magnificent, craggy mountain, suffers as much for the relative ease with which it can be attained from its col with Scafell Pike as for its proximity to the higher mountain.

Finally, if you enjoy days away from the struggling masses, lies Illgill Head, an elongated whaleback south west of the two Scafells. Sandwiched between Wasdale, to which it sends its sprawling screes, and tranquil, relatively unknown Miterdale, Illgill Head on a warm summer's day is as fine an excursion as any in Lakeland.

Route 7.1 Scafell Pike from Seathwaite Seathwaite Farm (235122) lies at the southern end of Borrowdale, and from it there are two excellent routes to Scafell Pike. Both are clear throughout, and each so full of interest, with constantly changing scenery, that to ascend by one and descend by the other leaves you with the satisfying replete feeling that comes from having feasted heartily. On the minus side, your legs will know they have been for a walk when you finally arrive back at Seathwaite.

Many are the choices of long hill days in the Lake District, but this circuit is unquestionably the finest, and should be reserved, like a *premier grand cru* wine, for that special occasion when the weather is fair and you are at your fittest. Tackle this on an off-day, and you will feel very jaded and disillusioned at the end of it!

7.1a By Esk Hause Leave Seathwaite heading south on the track between the farm buildings, and follow this uneventfully to Stockley Bridge (234109), a packhorse bridge partially demolished by floods in 1966, but now restored. Cross the bridge to a gate and turn left to follow a wall, ignoring the path ascending from the gate across rough ground to the hanging valley from which cascades Taylorgill Force; this is Route 7.1b.

The route to Esk Hause ascends gradually, following first Grains Gill (on the left) and later Ruddy Gill which is crossed, by a bridge, near its junction with Grains Gill. Ruddy Gill is recrossed in its upper reaches, beneath the towering rock buttresses of Great End, by boulder-hopping across a shallow ford. The immense gully-riven face of Great End provides some of the finest snow and ice climbing outside Scotland, and almost forces you over backwards as you gaze upwards.

Once across Ruddy Gill, scramble up the crumbly red earth (due to the presence of haematite) which gives the gill its name, and join a good track running north west–south east, linking Styhead Tarn with Esk Hause, a route dating back to Neolithic times. Follow this ancient pathway towards Esk Hause where first you encounter a stone shelter (which is at the top of the path ascending from Langdale – Route 7.2) before arriving finally, a short distance further on, at the true hause, unmarked apart from a line of cairns which guide you across this high pass into the sanctuary of Calf Cove (not named on the 1:50000 map). Calf Cove lies just south of Great End, which here has traded its craggy face for a much less severe posterior. If you don't want to visit the Esk Hause shelter – it offers a grand view of the Langdale Pikes and an easy scamper up nearby Allen Crags – you can take a short cut to Calf Cove (marked on the map) by leaving the Esk Hause path not long after you joined it at the top of Ruddy Gill and following a rugged, rising path, right, to reach Esk Hause near Calf Cove.

Walk into Calf Cove, where incidentally you will find the last running water on the ascent, and climb out of it by a loose scree path to gain the long connecting ridge between Great End and Ill Crag. Recent aerial surveys now show Ill Crag to be marginally higher than Broad Crag, so deposing the latter as the second of the three Scafell 'Pikes'. From the entrance to Calf Cove, Ill Crag displays a neat, conical shape, dominating its surround-

Scafell Pike from Ill Crag.

ings, and wishful thinking, mistaking this for Scafell Pike itself, could have you at the end of your journey sooner than expected. Alas, the awful truth dawns on you as you leave Calf Cove behind; Scafell Pike is still some distance away across the bouldery shoulders of both Ill Crag and Broad Crag.

Follow the path from Calf Cove, taking care crossing a bad stretch of large boulders, and descend to the col with Broad Crag. On the shoulder of Broad Crag, a summit whose rough and boulder-strewn proclivity has no equal in England, the path becomes vague, and is marked by a line of cairns. Follow this, passing a little way south of the summit, to the narrow, steep-sided col with Scafell Pike. Both Ill Crag and Broad Crag may be reached by simple, but rough, diversions from the path, though this is not recommended in mist.

Having reached the col with Scafell Pike, the final rough scramble to the summit will not deter you, but it can be tricky in winter conditions, and, in mist, the way back down to the col should be committed to memory before the euphoria of having reached the highest point in England overwhelms prudence: it isn't difficult to follow, but a proliferation of cairns makes it confusing at times.

No description of the summit view has been written to better that of Wordsworth:

On the summit of the Pike, which we gained after much toil, though without difficulty, there was not a breath of air to stir even the papers containing our refreshment, as they lay spread upon a rock. The stillness seemed to be not of this world: – we paused, and kept silence to listen; and no sound could be heard: the Scawfell Cataracts were voiceless to us; and there was not an insect to hum in the air. The vales which

Storm clouds brew over the Scafells. ▶

The Scafells and Crinkle Crags from Black Sails.

we had seen from Ash-course [Esk Hause] lay yet in view; and side by side with Eskdale we now saw the sister Vale of Donnerdale terminated by Duddon Sands. But the majesty of the mountains below, and close to us, is not to be conceived. We now beheld the whole mass of Great Gavel [Gable] from its base, – the Den of Wastdale at our feet – a gulf immeasurable; Grasmere and the other mountains of Crummock; Ennerdale and its mountains; and the Sea beyond!

DISTANCE: 6.5 kilometres (4 miles)
ASCENT: 920 metres (3020 feet)

7.1b By Sty Head and the Corridor Route Follow Route 7.1a to the gate just after Stockley bridge, but then continue ahead, climbing on an improved track to a gate in the intake wall. Here the path curves upwards to the top of Taylorgill Force, where Styhead Gill spills spectacularly into the glacial valley below. Continue, without difficulty, on a path running parallel with the gill, and later crossing it by a bridge.

The bridge may be reached from Seathwaite by a route both shorter and, in my opinion, vastly more entertaining, involving a little scrambling, but with a close view of the ravine into which Taylorgill Force falls. Leave the farm through the arch in the buildings on the right, and continue to a bridge across the River Derwent. Here turn left on a path that is occasionally wet, but improving as you start to climb to the waterfall. A little scrambling near the falls requires care, but beyond the going is easy.

A short distance beyond the bridge across Styhead Gill, where the Taylorgill Force path joins, Styhead Tarn springs into view against a breathtaking backdrop, especially impressive if you stand at the outflow of the tarn, of Great End, Broad Crag, Scafell Pike and Lingmell. The circle of mountains is completed on the right by the soaring bulk of Great Gable and, across the wide scree gully of Aaron Slack, Green Gable.

Resume the path to Sty Head. This, like Esk Hause, is a high mountain pass comparable with many in the Alps and the Pyrenees; the Mountain Rescue box you will find there reminds you that you are a long way from any outside help in an emergency.

From the pass pathways abound: north east runs the path you have just ascended; south east, skirting Great End, is the path to Esk Hause mentioned in Route 7.1a; north west, the path to the summit of Great Gable lures invitingly, while south of it the track to Kern Knotts and the Napes slants across Gable's lower slopes; west, descends the path to Wasdale, the route taken by the Four Passes Walk (Classic Walks 10).

The Corridor Route (once known as the Guides Route) is in view from Sty Head, but is not as immediately obvious as other paths. It links together a series of grassy shelves across the lower slopes of Great End and Broad Crag. To get on to it, either locate a faint grassy path from the mountain rescue box which intersects it, or take the Esk Hause path for a short distance until the start of the Corridor Route appears on the right. Either way the next hour will pass in a splendidly rugged area, unsurpassed in the whole of Lakeland.

Shortly after leaving Sty Head the Corridor Route encounters Skew Gill (not named on the 1:50 000 map), a narrow red gully of crumbly rock. As you leave the gully be sure to take the higher of two paths you find since the lower one, albeit the original route, leads into Greta Gill and involves some unpleasant scrambling to effect an escape. The upper path however continues pleasantly to the head of Greta Gill. The view across the valley to the north, down which flows Lingmell Beck, is truly spectacular, enhanced by the way the mountains of Mosedale – Yewbarrow, Red Pike, Scoat Fell, and finally Pillar – progressively emerge from behind the intervening dome of Kirk Fell. Great Gable dominates the scene

The Scafells, seen from the slope of Seatallan. The long, low ridge in the middle distance is Yewbarrow.

northwards, while the gullies of Lingmell, in particular Piers Gill, march nearer.

Continue on a good path until obviously faced with a choice of routes. Left, ascending to Broad Crag col, is a relatively new route not shown on maps, while to the right, the original way lies across the top of Piers Gill and on to Lingmell col. At Broad Crag col Route 7.1a is joined for the final pull to the summit, and this way is a little shorter than by Lingmell col, from where a line of cairns marks the way to the top.

DISTANCE: Shortest – 6.2 kilometres (3.9 miles); longest – 6.5 kilometres (4 miles)
ASCENT: 850 metres (2785 feet)

Having reached the summit of England with comparative ease, the continuation to the second highest summit presents more than enough problems to compensate. Walkers

Storm clouds gather over the crags of Scafell Pike (left) and Scafell. The long, ascending slope on the left leads to the top of Lingmell.

who have the least nervous disposition, or who feel intimidated by unstable rock and precarious situations should opt for the ascent of Scafell from Wasdale (Route 7.4) or over Slight Side (Route 7.6). The direct lines, involving Lord's Rake, Broad Stand or Foxes Tarn Path, are not routes to be undertaken lightly. If in doubt, retreat; the three options are bad enough going up, they are ten times worse coming down! On the other hand, if you are not easily intimidated, or are otherwise happy and competent on rock (including the loose, friable variety), then Scafell Pike to Scafell across the intervening Mickledore is an excellent mountaineering traverse, sufficiently so to merit separate description (see Route 7.8).

Route 7.2 Scafell Pike from Langdale One of the problems with Scafell Pike is that it is awkwardly situated in relationship to the main roadway links that bring walkers to the Lake District every weekend. The shortest ascent is from Wasdale, which involves by far the longest and most circuitous approach by car, while the finest ascent, from Seathwaite in my opinion, necessitates a tortuous and time-consuming drive down Borrowdale, particularly at the height of summer. For these reasons many walkers tackle Scafell Pike from Langdale, no less tortuous an approach for drivers than from Borrowdale, but more direct and making less demand on your time.

The ascent from Langdale, starting at the Old Dungeon Ghyll Hotel (286062), is long and rough, and for any but the strongest walkers affords no variant route by which to return. By way of compensation, if bad weather should compel you to abandon your original plans, there are sufficient, nearer summits otherwise passed en route to enable you to retrieve something from the day.

Leave the car park at Old Dungeon Ghyll by following the path round the back of the hotel building to a stile after which you gain the long established track through Mickleden. At the head of Mickleden cross Stake Gill (not named on the 1:50000 map), and take the left fork

At the head of Wastwater.

to ascend by a zig-zag route into Rossett Gill. Some walkers like to make heavy weather of Rossett Gill, but in spite of its reputation for toughness, it succumbs easily enough if you go at it at a steady 'talking' pace. From the top of Rossett Gill, continue ahead and down to the hollow containing Angle Tarn from where a loose, rising path takes you over the minor summit, Tongue Head, eventually to the shelter on Lower Esk Hause, where you join Route 7.1a to the summit. The whole of the approach through Mickleden and Rossett Gill is described in more detail in Route 2.5 in Volume Two, though it is never in doubt.

DISTANCE: 8 kilometres (5 miles)
ASCENT: 1015 metres (3330 feet)

Route 7.3 Scafell Pike from Eskdale All ascents of Scafell Pike are, as befits the highest mountain in England, long and tough. The approach through Eskdale is no exception, but can cause greater difficulty than the others in misty conditions.

Route 2.7 in Volume Two describes a number of variant ways to the Great Moss beneath Cam Spout Crag in upper Eskdale, and one of these should be used. It is also possible to take the track to Lingcove Bridge, then through Esk Gorge to emerge on a broad, boggy platform a short distance below Great Moss. This approach has the most continuous path, but even this peters out as you reach the Moss. It has the disadvantage however of keeping you on the wrong side of the river, which then has to be forded, an accomplishment which cannot always be achieved in wet weather.

As you reach Great Moss the splash of Cam Spout itself is usually noticeable on the mountainside, and alongside it a rough scree path which will take you strenuously up to Mickledore. From here follow the good path, right, to the summit of Scafell Pike.

DISTANCE: 7.7 kilometres (4.8 miles)
ASCENT: 890 metres (2920 feet)

Route 7.4 Scafell Pike from Wasdale The ascent from Wasdale is by far the shortest of the routes up Scafell Pike, and though Wasdale has, rightly, been a Mecca for rock climbers and fell-walkers for almost two hundred years, I would not rate this ascent as highly as any of the others. The customary line goes by Lingmell Gill to Lingmell Col, and is a little dreary, though it can be enhanced by tackling Lingmell first (see Route 7.11). An alternative is to meet the screes below Mickledore head on, and to make for the summit from there. This is much better, but more demanding on energy.

Begin at the car park near the camp site at the head of the lake, and follow a sign-posted route to a bridge crossing Lingmell Gill. Continue for a short distance to a gate where the path forks, the left route lumbering up Lingmell, while the right fork stays with the gill until, a little under a kilometre further on (about half a mile), you have to cross it by

The approach to Sty Head; Lingmell is the fell in the background.

boulder-hopping – tricky after prolonged rain or when the spring meltwaters are flowing fast. Once across the gill the track ascends roughly up the steep, eroded mound of Brown Tongue (not named on the 1:50 000 map) and later dividing, not too clearly, as you reach the edge of the amphitheatre known as Hollow Stones. The left fork takes a cairned route to Lingmell Col, ascending by a prominent path from there, while the right fork continues ahead, passing a broad fan of grey scree on your right which spills from the foot of Scafell Crag, and to a steep and badly eroded path leading to Mickledore. Here the route, though rocky, becomes infinitely easier to negotiate, and takes you, left, to Scafell Pike.

DISTANCE: 4 kilometres (2.5 miles) by Lingmell Col, and 3.7 kilometres (2.3 miles) by Mickledore
ASCENT: 910 metres (2985 feet)

Route 7.5 Scafell from Wasdale The fine ascent of Scafell from Wasdale ranks with the best Wasdale has to offer, and is far more rewarding than the companion ascent of Scafell Pike whose greater height is a predictable magnet for all walkers at some time or other. It is, of course, Lord's Rake that gives this route its appeal, far surpassing any attraction Broad Stand may have (in any event you have to be capable of scaling Broad Stand), and infinitely superior to the long, grassy plod up Green How, once much favoured by the Victorian explorers of this region.

Leave the car park at the head of the lake and follow a sign-posted path, a Permissive Path, courtesy of the Fell and Rock Climbing Club, to Hollow Stones (described in more detail in Route 7.4). As you reach Hollow Stones a wide splash of grey scree is prominent on the right, and this should be ascended, carefully (it's very loose), to the foot of Lord's Rake, near the cross carved in the rock, which I have mentioned in Route 7.8. This route is then followed to the summit, either by following the full length of the rake, or by pursuing the deviation up Deep Gill by the West Wall Traverse.

DISTANCE: 3.8 kilometres (2.4 miles)
ASCENT: 915 metres (3000 feet)

The alternative via Green How, the route taken by Coleridge when he made his epic descent of Broad Stand in 1802, is best reserved as a quick way down, but it is the key to Scafell for walkers who feel disinclined to tackle the few breaches in the mountain's north eastern defences.

From the same starting point proceed to a sign-post pointing the way to Eskdale close by Brackenclose (185073 – shown, but not named on the 1:50000 map), and follow the path thus indicated. The route, which serves also to gain Illgill Head from Wasdale, eventually leads by way of Burnmoor Tarn to Boot in Eskdale, but should be left a short distance after passing the intake

Lord's Rake: the second col. Scafell Pike and Pikes Crag are in the background.

wall to follow the line of a stream upwards to the summit.
DISTANCE: 3.2 kilometres (2 miles)
ASCENT: 900 metres (2950 feet)

Route 7.6 Scafell from Eskdale over Slight Side The long south ridge of Scafell careers to an abrupt halt at the neat summit of Slight Side, and though few walkers will make this the sole objective of a day out, it does occupy a fine position with extensive views of the coastal region.

Start from the small car park (200009) on the north side of the road, near Wha House Farm. Cross the nearby stile, and follow a path climbing to a group of sheepfolds constructed as part of the intake wall. Pass through these and follow the wall for a while, gradually climbing away from it through a splendid area of granite bumps and bracken-filled hollows. The route is always cairned when

Pikes Crag, better known as Pulpit Rock, is easily gained from the top of Scafell Pike, and gives a grandstand view of Scafell Crag and Lord's Rake. ▶

The start of the ascent of Lord's Rake (Scafell). ▶ ▶

Lord's Rake: the final section. Turn left at the top for the rocky pull to Scafell's summit.

it needs to be, and leads eventually to the gathering ground of Cowcove Beck, a large boggy expanse known as Quagrigg Moss. The path, less entertaining in this upper section, crosses the lower slopes of the Moss, finally arriving at the base of a line of cairns leading you to an energetic pull to the summit cairn.

DISTANCE: 4.4 kilometres (2.75 miles)
ASCENT: 670 metres (2200 feet)

The continuation to Scafell is delineated by the long escarpment on the right falling to the Great Moss in

◄ ◄ *Lord's Rake: this upward-tilted shot makes the first section of the Rake appear less severe than it is. The top few metres of this part are notoriously loose and dangerous.*

◄ *Lord's Rake: retrospective to the first col. The obvious col, distant right, is Mickledore.*

Upper Eskdale, the views down which do much to enliven an otherwise dull plod.

DISTANCE: 1.5 kilometres (0.9 miles)
ASCENT: 215 metres (705 feet)

Route 7.7 Scafell from Eskdale by Cam Spout Excursions into the hinterland of Eskdale, where the upper reaches of the River Esk flow contentedly across the Great Moss, are for the enthusiast more than the curious walker. It is a remarkable place where high crag, indeed the highest, and rugged moorland meet; where soaring heights ease themselves majestically from the surrounding terrain. Connoisseurs' country, a place where tales of daring mountain exploits are born and bred.

So far as the ascent of Scafell is concerned, there is little variation to the route for Scafell Pike described in Route 7.3. Only on ascending from Cam Spout to Mickledore do you deviate. Continue upwards from Cam Spout, as if making for Mickledore, but a short distance before the bulging belly of the East Buttress enter a prominent stony gully on the left. This, by a rough but direct line, will take you to Foxes Tarn, beyond which a badly eroded scree slope climbs to the summit plateau, from where the top of the mountain lies a short distance south.

DISTANCE: 7.5 kilometres (4.7 miles)
ASCENT: 875 metres (2870 feet)

Route 7.8 Scafell Pike and Scafell across Mickledore
The wide cleft of Mickledore separating Scafell Pike and Scafell is associated with a dyke of rock passing through it less resistant to the forces of weathering than those adjoining. Visually there is no question that something about Mickledore marks it as decidedly different in character and composition from England's highest mountains, though only a geologist would recognise just what. For walkers it is the only weakness in a massive wall of

steep crags and rugged ground that mail the flanks of both Scafells.

Many visitors to this high col, particularly those travelling from Scafell Pike to Scafell may be forgiven for feeling aggrieved that Mickledore, which so lures the walker from above, ends abruptly at a bold, impassable wall of rock when encountered at close hand. The more so because the path to Mickledore from Scafell Pike is easy to follow, setting off west from the summit for a short distance before swinging south west. And taking care not to wander mistakenly down the path to Lingmell col, which forks right from the Mickledore path not far from the top of the Pike, is the only problem you are likely to encounter. After that the rocky path continues without complication to Mickledore. In reverse, coming up from Mickledore is even simpler, not posing any doubt in pursuit of the correct course, which is well boot-marked throughout.

Problems arise at Mickledore however, there being no immediately obvious line of progression, nor, it has to be said, is there an easy one. The walker here is faced with three choices (four if you include packing up and going home!) – Lord's Rake, Broad Stand or the Foxes Tarn path. In all cases, in either direction, the distance and ascent are meaningless in computing how long the traverse will take; it all depends on your own stamina, resilience and courage!

Lord's Rake This remarkable feat of geological ingenuity crosses the north face of Scafell, almost literally rubbing your nose up against its towering precipices. At the best of times it must have been intimidating, but thousands of pairs of boots and sliding bottoms have taken their toll and for the most part it is now a treadmill of broken rocks, scree and loose earth calling for the utmost care. Rather like banging your head against a brick wall, it's lovely when you stop!

Cross Mickledore to the edge of Scafell Crag and there,

and not before, descend right down a badly eroded path keeping close to the base of the crags. This takes you to the foot of Lord's Rake, a broad, stone-filled gully, rising in a dead straight line, and sandwiched between the crags of Scafell and a subsidiary buttress on the right. At the start of the rake a cross carved in the rock commemorates the death of four climbers who in 1903 fell from the crags while reputedly attempting Owen Glynne Jones' Direct Route.

Continue into the base of Lord's Rake and scramble, uneasily at times, to the first obvious col, scarcely wide enough to stand on, clearly visible above. From here a short descent and re-ascent places you at a second col from where, some way ahead the end of the rake can be seen. A longish, eroded descent is again required before you can tackle the final escape from the rake, predictably up an eroded path. Once out of the rake, turn left and follow a rocky path upwards to a small plateau with the minor top, Symonds Knott (not named on the 1:50000 map) on your left. A branch path, heading right here, soon places you on the summit.

In reverse, especially in mist, two important things must be remembered. One, the location of the path descending to the top of Lord's Rake, and the fact, not obvious on the ascent, that a branch going left takes you not to Lord's Rake but out on to the wide open grassy expanse of Green How – a safe, fast way down, but not Lord's Rake. Secondly, it is vitally important to realise that the start of Lord's Rake is much lower down than you tend to imagine, and the gaping maw of Red Gill occurs first, tempting you astray. Red Gill and Lord's Rake do meet eventually, but the gill is notoriously bad in its upper section, and not so brilliant lower down!

Adventurous souls will rejoice in the West Wall Traverse alternative to a full ascent of Lord's Rake. This takes the chasm of Deep Gill which is entered just below the first col on Lord's Rake, by a narrow grassy path slanting left across the west wall of the gill, until, higher up, it moves into the gill proper for a final scrappy pull to the top, reaching the summit plateau with Symonds Knott on your right. The rock in its inner recesses is particularly friable, demanding the testing of each hand and foot hold before trusting to it.

Broad Stand The ascent of Broad Stand requires courage, conviction, strong arms and, ideally, someone's head to stand on. It begins with an exposed scramble, turning for a couple of awkward moves into serious rock-climbing, though serious rock climbers waltz up and down it with sickeningly casual aplomb, and ending with a scrambly ascent over rubble-strewn ledges and tracks.

The first person successfully to negotiate Broad Stand did so in August 1802 in a style that these days would be thought reckless, though we've all done the same sort of thing at some time or other, no doubt. It was Samuel Taylor Coleridge, who, in the following extract, is boasting to Sara Hutchinson, the girl he loved but was not free to marry:

I passed down from Broad-crag, skirted the Precipices, and found myself cut off from a most sublime Crag-summit, that seemed to rival Sca' Fell Man in height, & to outdo it in fierceness. A Ridge of Hill lay low down, & divided this Crag (called Doe-crag) & Broad-crag – even as the Hyphen divides the words broad & crag. I determined to go thither; the first place I came to, that was not direct Rock, I slipped down, & went on for a while with tolerable ease – but now I came (it was midway down) to a smooth perpendicular Rock about 7 feet high – this was nothing – I put my hands on the Ledge, & dropped down/in a few yards came just such another/*dropped* that too/and yet another, seemed not higher – I would not stand for a trifle/so I dropped that too/but stretching of the muscle[s] of my hands & arms, & the jolt of the Fall on my Feet, put my whole Limbs in a *Tremble*, and I paused, & looking down, saw that

I had little else to encounter but a succession of these little Precipices – it was in truth a Path that in a very hard Rain is, no doubt, the channel of a most splendid Waterfall. – So I began to suspect that I ought not to go on/but then unfortunately tho' I could with ease drop down a smooth Rock 7 feet high, I could not *climb* it/so go on I must/and on I went/the next 3 drops were not half a Foot, at least not a foot more than my own height/but every Drop increased the Palsy of my Limbs – I shook all over, Heaven knows without the least influence of Fear/and now I had only two more to drop down/to return was impossible – but of these two the first was tremendous/it was twice my own height, & the Ledge at the bottom was [so] exceedingly narrow, that if I dropt down upon it I must of necessity have fallen backwards & of course killed myself. My Limbs were all in a tremble . . .

Walkers who have attempted Broad Stand, up or down, and especially those who have failed, will understand exactly what Coleridge meant. The only footnote to this little episode is that it has since been argued, an argument to which I feel inclined to lend support, that it wasn't after all Broad Stand that Coleridge negotiated, but the nearby Mickledore Chimney: that's not taking anything away from Coleridge, the chimney is considerably more difficult.

The entrance, for that is just what it is, to Broad Stand lies a short distance down the Eskdale side of Mickledore, and is easily identified by a narrow rent in the rocks, aptly known as Fat Man's Agony. Squeeze into this to gain a narrow ledge, and then move left on polished holds to swing round on to a small bulge of rock, again with polished but adequate holds for hands and feet. Above, rising from a narrow platform, is an apparently innocuous corner scarcely higher than most people can reach. This is, in the language of the rock climber, 'the crux', for easy though the corner may seem, the dexterity and strength so essential to success are frequently thwarted by the general paucity of useful holds on the next platform above. Given someone's shoulders to stand on, it's no problem, unless they want to come up, too.

Above this modest dilemma, the route to Scafell rises by a well-trodden track, sufficiently cairned in its upper reaches to guide you safely on to it for the return journey. For the record, I consider the descent far more difficult than the ascent, it's certainly infinitely more intimidating.

Foxes Tarn path Descend further towards Eskdale than Broad Stand, passing en route the moss-lined Mickledore Chimney, and continue downwards to the foot of an obvious gully on the right which can be ascended without incident first to Foxes Tarn, really a muddy puddle with a large boulder in it, and then by badly eroded scree slopes and paths to the summit plateau. Again the upper reaches are well-cairned, and mark the line of descent, but I can't escape the feeling that whichever route you choose to ascend Scafell, save the easy ascents over Slight Side from Eskdale and Green How from Wasdale, a visit on a clear day, and probably more than one, to familiarise oneself with the topography is needed before less convenient conditions are faced up to.

By way of a short cut from the Foxes Tarn route, in descent, there is a narrow, cairned path skirting the foot of the massive, overhanging East Buttress, which saves a good deal of re-ascent. It leaves the Foxes Tarn path a short distance below the tarn, and starts by climbing left. If in doubt, continue down the main gully.

Route 7.9 Illgill Head and Whin Rigg Tucked away in the south west corner of Lakeland, these two summits, neither of them of special merit, form a short ridge, bounded on the south east by the rolling moorland of Eskdale, and on the north west by their saving grace, the magnificent Wastwater Screes. As a result, and most especially for the splendid, airy views that can be gained from their tops, the two fells, Illgill Head in particular, are worth the attention of every walker at some time during an exploration of the Lake District.

The most direct ascent, a simple one at that, leaves the car park at the head of Wastwater, as if making for the Scafells, but then pursuing the sign-posted track to Eskdale, an old corpse road, in fact. This takes you on to the broad splash of boggy ground north of Burnmoor Tarn from where a clear path can be seen rising up the north east corner of Illgill Head. A broken wall treks up most of this line, but does not continue to the summit cairn, which itself stands a short distance back from the edge of the screes, and gives no clue to the dramatic scenery but a short distance away.

DISTANCE: 4 kilometres (2.5 miles)
ASCENT: 545 metres (1790 feet)

The continuation to Whin Rigg is on the face of it dull, but by keeping as close as safety will allow to the escarpment, some truly thrilling views will be obtained.

DISTANCE: 2.3 kilometres (1.4 miles)
ASCENT: 60 metres (195 feet)

If the whole of the north east face of Illgill Head is of the most savage and rugged kind, the south west flank amply restores the balance, giving the fell a Jekyll and Hyde personality. For here you will find one of Lakeland's quietest and most attractive valleys, Miterdale. The valley is formed from that lovely pink Eskdale granite which, unlike harder rocks of Borrowdale Volcanic country, does not lend itself to spectacular scenery.

Miterdale is sign-posted from Eskdale Green, and motorable for half its length, but a walk in is, I feel, much preferable. As far as Low Place, the scenery is pastoral, reflective and a pleasure to pass through. Beyond Low

Lingmell Beck at the head of Wasdale. Kirkfell is the mountain on the right, and Red Pike, in the distance, is caught by the sun. ▶

Place, as you leave the trees behind, the valley narrows until there is barely room for the stream which flows through it. But as you approach its head it opens up quite dramatically into an unsuspected and impressive craggy amphitheatre of rocks and trees and miniature cascades. A path leads out of the amphitheatre on the left (true right) of the stream and places you within a few minutes of that isolated building, Burnmoor Lodge, overlooking its tarn. The path continues, above the tarn, towards Wasdale, and from it you can quite easily strike upwards for the summit of Illgill Head, or, if you prefer the security of a path, continue until you join the one mentioned above, coming up from Wasdale.

DISTANCE: 7.2 kilometres (4.5 miles) from Eskdale Green, by the shortest route, ascending directly from Burnmoor Tarn.

ASCENT: 550 metres (1805 feet)

There is something indefinably attractive about Burnmoor Tarn which is one of the largest mountain tarns in the Lake District. These lonely moors are reputedly haunted by the spirit of a horse which bolted, and was never recovered, while conveying a corpse across from Eskdale to Wasdale.

Route 7.10 Lingmell from Seathwaite The north face of Lingmell and the tremendous ravine of Piers Gill are as savage a scene of rock architecture as any you might find in the Lake District, and the summit of the mountain offers by far the best view of Great Gable. But of course it is its immediate neighbour, Scafell Pike, which draws all the attention, leaving walkers to visit Lingmell almost as an afterthought.

The ascent from Seathwaite simply follows Route 7.1b to Styhead, and along the Corridor Route to Lingmell col, from where a short descent and re-ascent west of north, crossing a collapsed wall en route, leads you to the rocky summit.

Lingmell, from the Corridor Route, which shows the savage gash of Pier's Gill to good advantage.

DISTANCE: 6 kilometres (3.75 miles)
ASCENT: 670 metres (2200 feet)

Route 7.11 Lingmell from Wasdale The graceful profile of Lingmell viewed from the head of Wasdale kids you into thinking it is but an easy stroll to gain its rocky summit. From one point of view it is, being a fairly constant, grassy slope with only one false summit to detract from some truly remarkable views. But the ascent is unrelenting, and just a shade too steep for comfort; it won't deter anyone, but such will be the state of your knees when you reach the top that somehow the breath-taking panorama across the lightning-like gash of Piers Gill to Sty Head, the Gables and Kirkfell becomes compulsory viewing.

Start from the car park, near the camp site at the head of the lake, and follow a sign-posted route, the Brown

Lingmell, across Lingmell Col. The ascent follows the grassy slope on the right.

Tongue/Hollow Stones route to the Scafells, over the bridge spanning Lingmell Gill. Ascend a short distance to a gate where the Scafells route continues ahead along the gill, and take a broad, green path heading left, up the long south west ridge of Lingmell. The route continues clearly, and without incident, except for the one false summit I mentioned, to the large cairn marking the highest point. Between Lingmell and the false summit a wall is met; in mist this will guide you safely to Lingmell col, should you need it, but otherwise plays no part in the ascent.

DISTANCE: 3 kilometres (1.9 miles)
ASCENT: 735 metres (2410 feet)

Route 7.12 Great End from Langdale This route is not so much a recommendation as an expression of the means by which you can reach Great End from Langdale; it is nevertheless a fine walk, better done out of season, when it is quieter. Most walkers passing this way are likely to be heading for the Scafells, and it is only at the very end of the walk that your secret comes out into the open: Great End is a worthy objective in itself.

Leave the car park at Old Dungeon Ghyll (286062), and pursue Route 2.5 (Volume Two) as far as Angle Tarn, which is always a good place to stop for a breather. At this point Route 2.5, making for the wide col high on your left, departs from the main trail which continues to the stone shelter on Lower Esk Hause. Follow this path, mostly of loose stones and becoming rather eroded, to the shelter, and there turn left, joining a broad path coming up (from your right) from Styhead and the top of Ruddy Gill. Stay on the path and cross the top of Esk Hause to enter a shallow corrie basin, Calf Cove (not named on the 1:50000 map). The path escaping from Calf Cove on the left leads eventually to Scafell Pike, but as soon as you

Great End, from Lingmell Col.

reach the top of it turn sharply right for the final short pull to the rocky summit plateau of Great End, on which there are two prominent cairns. The cairn nearest to Calf Cove (the south east) marks the highest point.

DISTANCE: 6.7 kilometres (4.2 miles)

ASCENT: 870 metres (2855 feet)

Misty conditions are not conducive to the exploration of Great End, but given a clear day and an absence of snow to mask any sudden drops, it is worth spending some time wandering around, not only for the splendid outward views, but for the exciting glimpses you can gain down the imposing gullies of Great End's north east face. But don't be tempted to descend any of them; there is a pedestrian route beyond the north west cairn which will lead you to Styhead, but the start of it isn't always easy to locate, and if you want to go that way it is safer to return to Esk Hause and take the track down from there; there is in any case a short cut from the top of Esk Hause to the top of Ruddy Gill (see Route 7.1a for details).

Route 7.13 Great End from Seathwaite The greater part of either of the two routes to Great End from Seathwaite is shared with lines of ascent to Scafell Pike. Route 7.1a takes you to Calf Cove via Grains Gill, Ruddy Gill and Esk Hause, where you then turn right, as described in Route 7.12 for the summit of Great End.

DISTANCE: 5.3 kilometres (3.3 miles)

ASCENT: 780 metres (2560 feet)

Great End from Esk Hause. ▲

The crags of Great End in winter give popular sport for the experienced climber. Even in summer they are a formidable proposition for anyone. ►

Seathwaite Fell and Sprinkling Tarn. ► ►

Route 7.1b takes you via Taylorgill Force to Styhead from where an ascending route, heading south eastward, takes you past the edge of Sprinkling Tarn and beneath the towering cliffs of Great End to join Route 7.1a at the top of Ruddy Gill, which can then be followed to Calf Cove.
DISTANCE: 6.3 kilometres (4 miles)
ASCENT: 780 metres (2560 feet)

In spite of the brief descriptions I have accorded these Routes, they are nevertheless both fine and interesting walking, and on a long summer's day could be combined with a trip across Esk Hause to Allen Crags and along the Glaramara ridge (Route 2.4 in Volume Two) before ending with a steep descent either to Seathwaite or Seatoller or, indeed, into Langstrath.

Route 7.14 Seathwaite Fell from Seathwaite Few walkers would consider visiting Seathwaite Fell as the sole objective of a day in the fells, but if you seek a quiet, pottering day then spare Seathwaite Fell a second thought. It is a humpy, hollowy, tarn-dappled summit, a northern continuation of Great End, which can easily fill a peaceful day.

Follow either the line of Grains Gill (Route 7.1a) to the crossing of Ruddy Gill, and there turn right (north west) until you reach the edge of Sprinkling Tarn. Or approach by Styhead Tarn, taking the south east route to Esk Hause, once again as far as Sprinkling Tarn. From the edge of the tarn, which literally laps the path, follow a narrow track along the north western shore which eventually will take you to the summit of Seathwaite Fell. The path however is not always clear, especially in mist

Esk Pike from Esk Hause. ▲

Esk Pike from the summit of Ill Crag. ▶

The boulder-strewn summit of Broad Crag.

when the numerous rocky buttresses and tarn-filled hollows can be confusing. As a rough guide, by no means foolproof, follow the path to the northern extremity of Sprinkling Tarn, and then head north for a short distance to another, smaller tarn with a sizeable dome of rock on your left. This can be mistaken for the summit, and is, in fact, only one metre lower in height. Continue ahead, still in a generally northerly direction, to an even smaller tarn beyond which rises the true summit, marked by a large cairn built on the top of a rocky outcrop.

DISTANCE: 4.5 kilometres (2.8 miles) by Grains Gill; 5 kilometres (3.1 miles) by Styhead Tarn.

ASCENT: 500 metres (1640 feet)

If you ascend by way of Stockley Bridge to the top of Taylorgill Force it is possible, once the gradient eases en route to Styhead Tarn, to find a way, left, across trackless ground to either of two fairly obvious grassy gullies breaching the rock face of Aaron Crags, which look down the length of the Seathwaite valley. This approach will bring you first to a very prominent cairn (229102) which it is tempting to think is the summit; but it isn't, and a short walk, west of south (about half a kilometre), is needed to find the true summit. By this route the distance can be reduced to 3 kilometres (1.9 miles), though the ascent is the same.

Section 8 – Dunnerdale and the Coastal Fells

	MAP REFERENCE	HEIGHT (m)	OS 1:50000 MAP
Dunnerdale			
Harter Fell	219997	653	96
The Coastal Fells			
Black Combe	135855	600	96
Whitfell	159930	573	96
Buck Barrow	152910	549	96

ROUTES

8.1   Harter Fell
8.2   Black Combe
8.3   Whitfell and Buck Barrow

Harter Fell, which dominates much of Dunnerdale, has long been popular with walkers, and rightly so, but it may surprise some to think of the seemingly innocuous coastal fells as part of Lakeland. Yet they are within the National Park boundary, they are partially comprised of the oldest rocks, Skiddaw Slates, in the region's geological history, the whole is an excellent, easy walking area and has as much claim as any other to be truly in keeping with the Lake District scene. Combined with adjacent Harter Fell it is a fine upland area, for is there, outside the central massif, a more ruggedly handsome summit than that of Harter Fell itself, or a more intriguing configuration of rocks than those of Buck Barrow, and where else will you find a summit that literally drags itself from the sea and arrays itself in so provocative a way as does Black Combe?

This splendidly wild tract of countryside richly repays the effort of getting to it. It is archaeologically rich, too, with stone circle remnants and cairns, especially the great stone circle at Swinside (172882), and the Giant's Grave at Kirksanton at Standing Stones farm (193873). Legend has it that the giant was killed in battle and buried in the tumulus and the last two upright stones seem to be survivors of a circle, suggesting a prehistoric interment. W. G. Collingwood writes: "This upland country was all wooded formerly, and before the middle of the twelfth century it was quite a no-man's land – neither England nor Scotland nor Cumbria proper; and so it would have been just the place for a sort of Adullam, a haunt of outlaws and sea-rovers, refugees and Viking squatters."

There is even now an air of mystery about the place, and the whole of it, not just the high fells, is an excellent alternative in the high season to popular routes elsewhere.

Route 8.1 Harter Fell Harter Fell is irresistible to anyone who knows the pull a mountain can exert on one's soul. It is from every direction a beautiful mountain, conspicuous in distant views from Whit Fell or Buck Barrow even against a backcloth of higher fells, a splendid pyramidal, forest-cloaked form when seen from the Duddon valley, and a fine, craggy challenge to anyone based near Boot or Wha House in Eskdale. And unlike some fells, its promise is fulfilled, especially in the charming approach from the north west.

8.1a From Eskdale Leave the Esk valley road at 189009 down a narrow roadway leading to the banks of the Esk. Cross the attractive Doctor Bridge spanning the river, and continue to Penny Hill farm, passing through the farmyard to gain a track running between walls. Follow the wall, passing through a gate, until a footpath sign-posted 'Harter Fell' departs, right, from the main track (which continues all the way to Hard Knott). Take the Harter Fell path, making for a corner of the intake wall, and then, through the second of two gates, follow this wall, taking care not to be misled by a prominent path leading to Kepple Crag (1:50000 sheet 96) – the correct way from the second gate is again sign-posted, though it is tempting, in view of the better state of the path you are on, to think someone has turned the sign the wrong way round!

Cross a narrow ravine (a good place to shelter on a blustery day) and traverse some marshy ground to ascend to an obvious gap between rocks ahead, where Harter Fell springs majestically into view. In spite of poor conditions underfoot the way ahead is clear enough, and crosses a fast-flowing stream, Spothow Gill (not named on the 1:50000 map), before finally getting to grips with Harter Fell itself. Once across the stream another path ascends from the left (the way up from Hard Knott or Wha House Bridge), though this is better as an alternative descent. Follow the path, which now is clear and, higher up, cairned all the way to the summit.

The summit arena is a bit confusing, having three prominent, rocky tops. A trig point, something you won't see until the last moment, adorns the most southerly, but it is quite obvious that a higher prominence looms nearby. It is the tip of this, a fine, rocky point which is the summit, but to get to it, at first glance, requires rock-climbing skills. Tackle it direct by all means, but an easy alternative lies around the back, enabling even the most timid walker to reach the very top of this splendid fell. The third summit lies a short distance east, and is the lowest.

DISTANCE: 3.6 kilometres (2.25 miles)
ASCENT: 585 metres (1920 feet)

8.1b From Birks Bridge

The ascent from Birks Bridge (234993) in the Duddon valley is a shorter, sharper alternative, but no less attractive, offering fine views of the Coniston fells.

Leave the Birks Bridge car park from where various routes through the Dunnerdale Forest, which cloaks this side of Harter Fell, are colour-coded. The summit route is clearly marked through the forest, and leads to a gully before reaching the open fellside. From the edge of the forest a good path ascends all the way to the summit.

DISTANCE: 1.8 kilometres (1.1 miles)
ASCENT: 470 metres (1540 feet)

The alternative ascent from the top of the Hardknott Pass is so insulting to this fine fell that I don't propose to give it any more space, while the approach via Grassguards in the Duddon valley (also accessible from the Birks Bridge car park), once, long ago, a promising second string, is now substantially afforested, and has bowed out in favour of Route 8.1b.

Route 8.2 Black Combe There is, so W. G. Collingwood tells us, an old Furness saying: "Nowt good ever comes round Black Combe!" No doubt it is a view stemming from pre-football days when raiding rather than rioting was the in-sport. Ambleside folk used to say the same of anyone crossing Dunmail Raise from Cumberland. Be that as it may, Black Combe is excellent walking country, and from its hoary summit in distant wardening days I once accomplished the most unusual mountain rescue of the year by carrying back to Whicham tucked inside my anorak what at first glance had been just another iced rock in the enormous cairn adorning the southern summit, in reality a sad and sorry cat that had somehow found its way on to the fell, and would surely have died had I not chanced along.

There are a number of routes crossing Black Combe, but that most in favour, and rightly so, starts from Whicham (135827). A narrow road leaves the A595 to give access to Whicham church and what used to be the

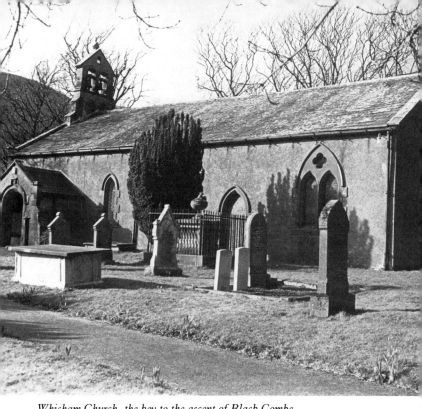

Whicham Church, the key to the ascent of Black Combe.

schoolroom. Pass between the two buildings to gain a minor road to Kirkbank (don't take cars, there is no parking space and no room to turn). Continue behind the building to gain the open fellside through a gate or a stile just outside the intake wall. A good path now climbs steadily all the way to the summit, which seems further than it is, but it is a splendid airy route. Finally, as the path noticeably starts to descend, at a left bend, another, less prominent, track climbs the adjoining shoulder, right, and leads directly to the trig point and stone shelter marking the highest point.

DISTANCE: 3.5 kilometres (2.2 miles)

ASCENT: 570 metres (1870 feet)

It is important, in misty conditions, to remember that the summit of Black Combe possesses a trig point. I say this because a short distance south, beyond the small tarn marked on the 1:50 000 map, the southern summit boasts one of the most magnificent cairns in the whole of Lakeland, the one from which I rescued the cat. It is tempting to look on this edifice as the natural adornment of the highest point; it isn't.

The main path across Black Combe eventually wends a way westward, back to the A595, which it joins at 112865. You can ascend from this direction, the start is sign-posted, and the route obvious. It is a little shorter, and involves marginally less ascent, but there is not much to commend it. Similarly, the ascent from Corney Fell Road, at 149897, is just so much moorland bog-bashing if you pick the wrong line across the trackless terrain. It would be excellent on skis.

Route 8.3 Whitfell and Buck Barrow North of Black Combe the grassy moorland rolls on towards Eskdale and Harter Fell, and, with a bit of imagination, provides an excellent high level approach to central Lakeland. Between Black Combe and the concealed, and almost forgotten Devoke Water, rise two major fells each with an attendant, providing escapees from summertime crowds with enough of a refuge to make the journey worthwhile.

The best approach is from the highest point of Corney Fell Road crossing the whaleback ridge at 149897. There is ample room to park here, and heading northwards a semi-derelict wall leads virtually to the very summit of Buck Barrow, passing two hundred metres west of the highest point, marked by a small cairn on a tiny plateau amid a marvellous upthrust of rocks.

DISTANCE: 1.7 kilometres (1 mile)
ASCENT: 150 metres (490 feet)

Nearby, to the west, Kinmont Buck Barrow is similarly crowned with rock outcrops, giving the two summits an

Buckbarrow and Whitfell from Corney Fell Road.

appearance not unlike Bera Mawr and Bera Bach in the Carneddau of North Wales.

Further north, across trackless boggy ground, the worst of which can be avoided, lies Whitfell, its summit marked by a shelter cairn and trig point, and affording a grand view northwards to the high mountains of central Lakeland.

DISTANCE: 2.2 kilometres (1.4 miles)
ASCENT: 9.5 metres (310 feet)

South west of Whitfell, Burn Moor, a flat grassy plateau, the highest point marked by a cairn at 151925, offers an easy extension, to be included either travelling to or from Whitfell.

Approaching the summit of Buckbarrow, one of the remote coastal fells. ▶

Kinmont Buckbarrow from the summit of Buckbarrow.

Approaching Whitfell.

Harter Fell from the Duddon valley.

Classic Walks

The walks contained in the preceding eight sections vary in strenuousness, and cater for all abilities, prevailing weather conditions, or time available. And though some have challenging moments, few are unduly long or difficult.

Anyone with enterprise, energy and the fundamental skills of map-reading and navigation will easily think of ways of linking many of these walks together to give longer days out on the fells. Indeed, in many ways, the compact nature of the Lake District almost demands this.

So, here, by way of a finale are ten classic longer distance walks based on routes already described:

1 The traverse of Skiddaw, Great Calva and Blencathra, from Keswick to Threlkeld
2 The Braithwaite Horseshoe
3 The Gasgale Watershed
4 The Newlands Horseshoe
5 The High Stile ridge
6 The Buttermere Horseshoe
7 The Ennerdale Horseshoe
8 The Mosedale Horseshoe
9 The Head of Wasdale
10 The Four Passes Walk

1 Skiddaw, Great Calva and Blencathra This is not a natural line, but it has a certain satisfaction for walkers who don't mind a bit of moorland wandering. It is also the first (or last) section of that Lakeland classic, the Bob Graham Round, which challenges walkers to complete a distance of 115 kilometres (72 miles) over 42 fells within 24 hours.

Ascend Skiddaw (Little Man is an optional extra) by Route 1.1, and continue northwards beyond the summit to descend to a slight depression about 700 metres further on. Then, leaving the path, descend, right, to cross a fence-line and continue downwards, aiming for the track to Skiddaw House about 1 kilometre (0.6 miles) north of the house.

The stretch from the track to the summit of Great Calva has a great abundance of heather of the high frustration factor variety. You will need to pick your way carefully through this to reach the southern summit of Great Calva, from where it is but a short walk to the highest point.

Return to the southern summit and descend through more heather to cross the River Caldew about one kilometre north east of Skiddaw House. You will probably have to wade across, depending on the time of year you choose; early spring is the worst time!

Once across the Caldew plod steadily up Mungrisdale Common, making for the left end of Blencathra, which now lies directly ahead. Ascend the scree path to the top of Foule Crag, marked by a large cairn, and cross easy ground southwards to the summit of Blencathra. Descend, leisurely I suggest, by Hall's Fell ridge (Route 1.7 in reverse).

DISTANCE: 19.2 kilometres (12 miles)
ASCENT: 1550 metres (5085 feet)

2 The Braithwaite Horseshoe For many walkers this circuit starts at the village of Braithwaite, hence the name, but the long, comparatively dull, grassy and heathery ridge of Sleet How, is something I prefer to be coming down at the end of a day rather than plodding up at the start. Undertaking the walk in clockwise direction, beginning at Stonycroft, has the advantage of getting you high on a quick succession of fells early on, and of having the strongest light in the best position for photographs.

Start from a small lay-by at 233222 on the Newlands valley road, a short distance north of Stonycroft, and use Route 2.4 to take you in fine style over Causey Pike, Scar Crags, Sail and Crag Hill. Continue to Coledale Hause by heading first for the col between Crag Hill and Grasmoor, and from the Hause aim for the slanting path to the unnamed summit south west of Grisedale Pike, and so on to the Pike itself.

Take care descending to Sleet How, especially in wet conditions, but after the initial steepness it is a fine romp to Braithwaite, from where you can follow a footpath to Braithwaite Lodge (233232) and back to the starting point.

DISTANCE: 10.6 kilometres (6.6 miles)
ASCENT: 1210 metres (3970 feet)

3 The Gasgale Watershed As its name suggests, this route pursues all the high ground that circles Gasgale Gill; it is a most delightful walk in spite of a strenuous start and a potentially tricky finish. Don't be misled by the apparent shortness of it. If you have skill with an ice-axe and can descend ice-covered slopes safely, this would make an excellent winter excursion on a bright, clear day.

Start by tackling Whin Ben, as described in Route 2.6, and continue to Whiteside, and along the ensuing ridge to Hopegill Head. Then over Sand Hill to Coledale Hause, from where, if necessary, you can escape down Gasgale Gill. Press on from the hause to the high col between Crag Hill and Grasmoor, and then take the broad path to the summit plateau of Grasmoor. Descend from Grasmoor by Lad Hows to Cinderdale Common; it is here, in the steep upper section, that you may encounter difficulties in winter.

DISTANCE: 9 kilometres (5.6 miles)
ASCENT: 935 metres (3065 feet)

As an alternative to descending by Lad Hows, you can return from Grasmoor to the col with Crag Hill, and then make for Wandope and Whiteless Pike, arriving at Cinderdale Common through Rannerdale (see Route 2.10b). Of course, this takes you off the Gasgale Watershed.

4 The Newlands Horseshoe I have already suggested in the text the delightful mini-horseshoe which starts at Rigg Beck and ascends Scope End to Hindscarth and descends from Robinson by High Snab Bank (see Routes 3.2 and 3.4), but the route described here is a much longer undertaking, an excellent high level walk. It starts at Hawes End, north east of Skelgill, and finishes at Rigg Beck; the two points are 2.2 kilometres (1.4 miles) apart.

From Hawes End (247212) take directly to the fellside to the south, ascending over Brandlehow and Cat Bells, and then on by Maiden Moor to High Spy. From High Spy descend to Dalehead Tarn, and pass round the tarn to start the steep, rough pull to the summit of Dale Head. Continue to Hindscarth and Robinson before descending across Buttermere Moss to Newlands Hause. Here, on

the last leg, trot up Knott Rigg and Ard Crags, descending to Rigg Beck over Aikin Knott.
DISTANCE: 18 kilometres (11.25 miles)
ASCENT: 1430 metres (4690 feet)

There are, of course, many escape routes from this walk should they be necessary; from Dalehead Tarn north into the upper Newlands valley, from Hindscarth down Scope End, from Robinson down High Snab Bank, and from Newlands Hause down the road north eastwards.

5 The High Stile ridge I have alluded in the main text to the quality of this fine ridge walk. Unlike most ridge walks it has the curious distinction of being accessible from a central valley base, Buttermere, nor does it much matter which way round you tackle it, though I tend to prefer east to west.

Start down the track passing by the Fish Hotel in Buttermere, and as you reach Burtness Wood follow the shore path, left (south east) to the end of the lake. Ascend to Scarth Gap, and then by Gamlin End to High Crag and the start of the ridge proper. After the assault of Gamlin End what follows is sheer delight.

Continue, easily now, to High Stile, the highest point of the ridge, and on to Red Pike, before descending to Starling Dodd and Great Borne, returning to Buttermere by Floutern Tarn and Scale Force (see Route 4.2).
DISTANCE: 19.3 kilometres (12 miles)
ASCENT: 965 metres (3165 feet)

The safest escape from the ridge back to Buttermere is from the summit of Red Pike.

6 The Buttermere Horseshoe My concept of the Buttermere Horseshoe does not marry up with that undertaken each year by fell-runners, the latter being an exquisite blend of agony, desperation and purgatory, mainly because it starts further west than my version (at

Loweswater), involves a distance of 32 kilometres (20 miles) and ascent of 2440 metres (8000 feet), and throws in innocuous trifles like Grasmoor and Mellbreak just for spite. The top runners, by the way, knock that off in under four hours! The route described here starts and finishes at Buttermere.

So, start by ascending Robinson, Hindscarth and Dale Head. Descend to the top of the Honister Pass and cross by the old road to Dubs Quarry to gain Hay Stacks (Route 4.6c). From Hay Stacks drop to Scarth Gap, and then tackle the High Stile ridge, returning to Buttermere by Floutern Tarn and Scale Force.

DISTANCE: 27 kilometres (17 miles)
ASCENT: 1830 metres (6000 feet)

Escapes are from the top of the Honister Pass, through Warnscale Bottom, from Scarth Gap, and from Red Pike summit.

7 The Ennerdale Horseshoe The full Ennerdale Horseshoe is quite a day out, the sort of thing over which you could spend four very acceptable days in the normal course of events. However, there is that species of humanity (and I'm one of them) who see no point in doing things the easy way when there is a much harder alternative, and so this delectable tit-bit of Lakeland is just for them. Don't even attempt to tell folks at home what time you'll be back!

Start at Whins farm (099167), about two kilometres (1.25 miles) from where you will finish, and follow Route 4.7 to the summit of Great Borne. If Steel Brow hasn't knackered you already, continue over Starling Dodd, Red Pike, High Stile, High Crags, Scarth Gap and Hay Stacks.

From Hay Stacks, aim to the right of Innominate Tarn and stay on the watershed to the top of Loft Beck (not named on the 1:50000 map), heading for Brandreth. From Brandreth head for Green Gable, then Great Gable and Kirk Fell, descending to the top of the Black Sail

Pass. Continue up Pillar (you might as well add Looking Stead, for good measure), and across Wind Gap to the unnamed summit, followed by Little and Great Scoat Fells and Haycock.

Leave Haycock for Little Gowder Crag and Caw Fell, and there follow the wall to and across Iron Crag to the forestry plantations spanning the col between Iron Crag and Crag Fell. Cross Crag Fell, and descend by Ben Gill to the lake shore. Collapse quietly!

DISTANCE: 33 kilometres (21 miles)
ASCENT: 2510 metres (8235 feet)

Escapes are from Scarth Gap, Windy Gap (between the two Gables), and Black Sail Pass. There are other options, but they are not inviting. You can, of course, abridge the route by short-cutting from Scarth Gap to the top of the Black Sail Pass, but I'm sure no one would ever contemplate doing that!

8 The Mosedale Horseshoe There are a number of Mosedales in Lakeland, but none quite match that off the head of Wasdale for spectacular walking. The task is simply to complete the round of the cirque, sticking to the watershed all the way, but I like to add Yewbarrow at the end, even though it has only a tenuous foothold in Mosedale.

Start from the hotel at Wasdale Head and head for Sty Head; don't be side-tracked by the sign pointing across a stone bridge to Mosedale. On approaching the foot of Kirk Fell, purists will tackle the fell head on, by the path soaring up the south west shoulder, but I wouldn't commend that to anyone. It makes infinitely more sense to continue along the track towards Sty Head, leaving it at a wooden bridge (199093) to ascend by Moses' Trod to Beck Head, and gaining the double-topped summit of Kirk Fell from there (Route 5.9c).

Descend from Kirk Fell to the top of Black Sail Pass, and follow a dilapidated fence-line to Pillar, deviating just a little to take in Looking Stead, which is an excellent vantage point for Ennerdale and the high level route to Pillar Rock.

Move on from Pillar, across Wind Gap, to the unnamed summit, and on to Scoat Fell, with its summit cairn perched on top of the wall. From Scoat Fell (Little Scoat Fell, in fact) head south east to conquer Red Pike, and from there descend to Dore Head beneath Yewbarrow's north east top, Stirrup Crag. Again purists will opt out here by descending easily, if steeply, to Mosedale. Walkers with more time on their hands will delight in the scrambly scamper to the top of Stirrup Crag, and along the ridge of Yewbarrow, descending steeply to Overbeck Bridge.

DISTANCE: 14 kilometres (8.75 miles)
ASCENT: 1450 metres (4755 feet)

9 The Head of Wasdale I've argued elsewhere in this book that Scafell Pike doesn't have a foothold in Wasdale, but I've no intention of leaving it out of this splendid circuit. I could also contend that since Kirk Fell appears as part of the Mosedale Horseshoe I could omit it from the Wasdale equivalent. But I'm not going to do that either!

All the walks I have described in this section can be undertaken clockwise or anti-clockwise, though I have described them in the way I feel does them best justice. With the Wasdale circuit it is virtually impossible to express any preference, both directions are superb. Why not do it one way one day, and the other the next?

The summits involved are Kirk Fell, Great Gable to Sty Head, Great End, Broad Crag (include Ill Crag for good measure), Scafell Pike and Scafell. If you start and finish at the car park near the camp-site at the head of the lake the distance and ascent must be the same whichever direction you choose.

DISTANCE: 15.5 kilometres (9.7 miles)
ASCENT: 1825 metres (5985 feet)

Those distances and ascents assume a direct ascent of Kirk Fell, ascending Great End by Calf Cove, crossing from Scafell Pike to Scafell by Broad Stand, and descending from Scafell by Green How.

10 The Four Passes Walk This is *the* long walk for days when the tops are shrouded in mist and you have itchy feet. You can start and finish at any of the valley bottoms though I customarily tackle it from Seatoller; nor does it matter much which way round you go.

So, Seatoller to Seathwaite and then to Sty Head, the first pass. Descend to Wasdale, but only to turn right into Mosedale to ascend to the top of the Black Sail Pass. Drop down to the head of Ennerdale, to the Black Sail Youth Hostel, and scamper along the edge of the forest to the third pass, Scarth Gap. Descend to Gatescarth at the end of Buttermere, and plod up and over the Honister Pass to return to Seatoller.

DISTANCE: 22 kilometres (13.75 miles)
ASCENT: 1230 metres (4035 feet)

On a clear day, from the top of Scarth Gap you can complete the circuit, omitting the plod up Honister, by linking the two passes across Hay Stacks and via the Dubs quarry. This is an excellent variation, which reduces the distance and the ascent.

Bibliography

Archaeological Sites of the Lake District, T. Clare (Moorland Publishing Co., 1981)

A Complete Guide to the English Lakes, Harriet Martineau (John Garnett, Windermere, 1855)

A Concise Description of the English Lakes, Jonathan Otley (Published by the author, Keswick, 1823)

A Description of the Scenery of the Lakes, William Wordsworth (Longman, Hurst, Rees, Orme, and Brown, 1823, Fourth Edition)

The Folklore of the Lake District, Marjorie Rowling (B. T. Batsford Ltd., London, 1976)

The Geology of the Lake District, J. E. Marr (Cambridge University Press, 1916)

Guide to the Lake District, Herman Prior (Simpkin Marshall & Co., London, 2nd Edition)

Guide to the Lakes, William Wordsworth (OUP, Fifth Edition, 1835)

The High Fells of Lakeland, Walt Unsworth (Robert Hale, 1972 and Cicerone Press, 1982)

The History of the County of Cumberland, William Hutchinson (F. Jollie, 1794)

The Lake Counties, W. G. Collingwood (J. M. Dent and Sons Ltd., 1902)

The Lake District, Roy Millward and Adrian Robinson (Eyre and Spottiswoode, London, 1970)

The Lake District, W. H. Pearsall and W. Pennington (Collins, 1973)

The Lakers – The First Tourists, Norman Nicholson (Robert Hale, 1955)

The Lakes of England, George Tattersall (Sherwood & Co., London, and Hudson and Nicholson, Kendal, 1836)

Land of the Lakes, Melvyn Bragg (Secker and Warburg, London, 1983)

Leigh's Guide to the Lakes (Leigh & Co., London, 1840)

Life and Tradition in the Lake District, William Rollinson (Dalesman Books, 1981)

Mountain Ascents in Westmorland and Cumberland, John Barrow FRS (Sampson Low, Marston, Searle & Rivington, London, 1886)

The Pictorial Guides to the Lakeland Fells, A. Wainwright (Westmorland Gazette, Kendal, 1955–1966, Seven volumes)

Rock Climbing in the English Lake District, Owen Glynne Jones (G. P. Abraham & Sons, Keswick, 1900 and E. J. Morten, Manchester, 1973)

Tales and Legends of the English Lakes, Wilson Armistead (Simpkin Marshall & Co., London, 1891)